Jacques Rancière

agreement

AND PHILOSOPHY

Translated by Julie Rose

University of Minnesota Press   Minneapolis   —   London

The University of Minnesota gratefully acknowledges financial assistance provided by the French Ministry of Culture for the translation of this book.

The publication of this book was assisted by a bequest from Josiah H. Chase to honor his parents, Ellen Rankin Chase and Josiah Hook Chase, Minnesota territorial pioneers.

This project has been assisted by the Commonwealth Government of Australia through the Australia Council, its arts funding and advisory body.

Copyright 1999 by the Regents of the University of Minnesota

Originally published as *La Mésentente: Politique et philosophie,* copyright 1995 Éditions Galilée.

Published by the University of Minnesota Press
111 Third Avenue South, Suite 290
Minneapolis, MN 55401-2520
http://www.upress.umn.edu

Library of Congress Cataloging-in-Publication Data

Rancière, Jacques.
[Mésentente, English]
Disagreement : politics and philosophy / Jacques Rancière ; translated by Julie Rose.
p.   cm.
Includes bibliographical references and index.
ISBN 978-0-8166-2844-5 (hc : alk. paper)
ISBN 978-0-8166-2845-2 (pb : alk. paper)
1. Political science — Philosophy.   I. Title.
JA71.R25513   1998
320'.01'1 — dc21
98-42205

Printed in the United States of America on acid-free paper

The University of Minnesota is an equal-opportunity educator and employer.

16 15 14 13 12 11 10 09 08   10 9 8 7 6 5 4 3 2

Contents

Preface

The question we must bear in mind is, equality or inequality in what sort of thing? For this is a problem, and one for which we need political philosophy.

Aristotle, Politics, *1282 b 21*

Is there any such thing as political philosophy? The question seems incongruous for two reasons. First, theorizing about community and its purpose, about law and its foundation, has been going on ever since our philosophical tradition kicked off and has never ceased to keep it vital. Second, for a while now, political philosophy has been loudly trumpeting its return with a new lease on life. Cobbled for a long time by Marxism, which turned the political into the expression, or mask, of social relationships, subject to poaching by the social and the social sciences, today, with the collapse of state Marxisms and the end of utopias, political philosophy is supposed to be finding its contemplative purity in the principles and forms of a politics itself returned to its original purity thanks to the retreat of the social and its ambiguities.

This return poses a few problems, however. When not limited to commenting on certain texts, famous or forgotten, from out of its own history, this rejuvenated political philosophy seems most unwilling to go beyond the usual assortment of arguments trotted out by any state administration in thinking about democracy and the law, right and the legitimate state. In short, the main aim seems to be to ensure communication between the great classic doctrines and the usual forms of state legitimization we know as liberal democracies. But the supposed convergence between the return of political philosophy and the return of its object, politics, is lacking in evidence. At a time when the political was contested in the name of the social, of social movements or social science, it was nonetheless still manifest in the multiplicity of modalities and places, from the street to the factory to the university. The resurrection of the political is today revealed in the discretion of such modalities or the absence of such places. One may object that the whole point is that politics purged has once again found the proper place for deliberation and decision-making concerning the common good, in assemblies where discussion and legislation take place, spheres of state where decisions are made, supreme courts that check whether such deliberations and decisions conform to the laws on which society is based. The problem is that these are the very places where the disenchanted opinion spreads that there isn't much to deliberate and that decisions make themselves, the work proper to politics simply involving an opportune adaptability in terms of the demands of the world marketplace and the equitable distribution of the profits and costs of this adaptability. The resurrection of political philosophy thus simultaneously declares itself to be the evacuation of the political by its official representatives.

This curious convergence obliges us to backtrack to political philosophy's *évidence première*. That there has (almost) always been politics *in* philosophy in no way proves that political philosophy is a natural offshoot of the tree of philosophy. Even in Descartes politics is not listed among the branches of the tree, medicine and morality apparently covering the field wherever other philosophies encountered politics. The first person in our tradition to come up against politics, Plato, only did so in the form of a radical exceptionality. As a philosopher, Socrates never reflected on the politics of Athens. He is the only Athenian to "do politics," to be involved in politics *in truth* as opposed to all that is done in Athens in the name of politics.[1] The first encounter between politics and philosophy is that of an alternative: either the politics of the politicians or that of the philosophers.

The starkness of this Platonic disjunction thus clarifies what remains apparent in the ambiguous relationship between the assurance of our political philosophy and the discretion of our politics. There is nothing to say that political philosophy is a natural division of philosophy, accompanying politics with its theory, however critical. In the first place there is nothing to say that any such philosophical configuration comes along and either echoes through theory or founds through legislation all the great forms of human acting — scientific, artistic, political, or otherwise. Philosophy does not have divisions that then lend themselves either to the basic concept proper to philosophy or to areas where philosophy reflects on itself or on its legislation. Philosophy has peculiar objects, nodes of thought borne of some encounter with politics, art, science, or whatever other reflective activity, that bear the mark of a specific paradox, conflict, aporia. Aristotle points this out in a phrase that is one of the first encounters between the noun *philosophy* and the adjective *political:* "Equality or inequality, comes down to aporia and political philosophy."[2] Philosophy becomes "political" when it embraces aporia or the quandary proper to politics. Politics, as we will see, is that activity which turns on equality as its principle. And the principle of equality is transformed by the distribution of community shares as defined by a quandary: when is there and when is there not equality in things between who and who else? What are these "things" and who are these whos? How does equality come to consist of equality *and* inequality? That is the quandary proper to politics by which politics becomes a quandary for philosophy, an object of philosophy. We should not take this to mean that pious vision in which philosophy comes to the rescue of the practitioner of politics, science, or art, explaining the reason for his quandary by shedding light on the principle of his practice. Philosophy does not come to anyone's rescue and no one asks it to, even if the rules of etiquette of social demand have established the habit whereby politicians, lawyers, doctors, or any other body getting together to reflect, wheel in the philosopher as specialist of thinking in general. If that invitation is to bear any intellectual fruit, the encounter must identify its point of disagreement.

We should take disagreement to mean a determined kind of speech situation: one in which one of the interlocutors at once understands and does not understand what the other is saying. Disagreement is not the conflict between one who says white and another who says black. It is the conflict between one who says white and another who also says white but does not understand the same thing by it or does not understand that the other is saying the same thing in the name of whiteness. The term is so broad it obviously calls for a certain amount of fine-tuning and obliges us to make certain distinctions. Disagreement is not misconstruction. The concept of misconstruction supposes that one or other or both of the interlocutors do or does not know what they are saying or what the other is saying, either through the effects of simple ignorance, studied dissimulation, or inherent delusion. Nor is disagreement some kind of misunderstanding stemming from the imprecise nature of words. Ancient received wisdom, very much in vogue again these days, deplores the way people fail to understand each other properly because of the ambiguity of the words exchanged, and requires us always, at all times, or at least wherever truth, justice, and good are at stake, to try and give each word a well-defined meaning, one that distinguishes it from all other words, discarding words that do not designate any defined property or that inevitably lead to homonymic confusion. It sometimes happens that this wisdom goes by the name of philosophy and manages to pass off this rule of linguistic economy as philosophy's privileged exercise. The reverse also happens, whereby philosophy is denounced as the very thing that promotes empty words and irreducible homonyms; every human activity, this wisdom goes, should get clear about itself, purging its vocabulary and conceptual underpinnings of all philosophy's bilge.

The arguments of misconstruction and misunderstanding thereby call for two types of language medicine, both consisting similarly in

finding out what speaking means. It is not hard to see their limita-
tions. The first type of treatment constantly has to assume the ignorant misconstruction of which it is the flip side, reserved knowledge.
The second imposes a rationality ban on too many areas. Numerous
speech situations in which reason is at work can be imagined within a
specific structure of disagreement that has neither to do with a misconstruction that would call for additional knowledge nor with a misunderstanding that would call for words to be refined. Disagreement occurs
wherever contention over what speaking means constitutes the very rationality of the speech situation. The interlocutors both understand and
do not understand the same thing by the same words. There are all sorts
of reasons why X both does and does not understand Y: while clearly
understanding what Y is saying, X cannot *see* the object Y is talking
about; or else, X understands and is bound to understand, sees and attempts to make visible another object using the same name, another
reason within the same argument. Thus, in the *Republic*, "political philosophy" comes into existence in the long protocol of disagreement over
an argument in which everyone agrees: that justice consists in giving
each his due. It would no doubt be convenient if, to say just what he
understands by justice, the philosopher had entirely different words at
his disposal from those of the poet, the merchant, the orator, or the
politician. Divine wisdom apparently did not provide these, and the
lover of strict and appropriate languages can furnish them only at the
cost of not being understood at all. Where philosophy runs up against
poetry, politics, and the wisdom of honest merchants, it has to borrow
the others' words in order to say that it is saying something else entirely.
It is in this that disagreement lies and not mere misunderstanding, which
can be resolved by a simple explanation of what the other's sentence is
saying — unbeknownst to this other.

Disagreement clearly is not to do with words alone. It generally bears
on the very situation in which speaking parties find themselves. In this,
disagreement differs from what Jean-François Lyotard has conceptualized as a differend.[3] Disagreement is not concerned with issues such as
the heterogeneity of regimes of sentences and the presence or absence

of a rule for assessing different types of heterogeneous discourse. It is less concerned with arguing than with what can be argued, the presence or absence of a common object between X and Y. It concerns the tangible presentation of this common object, the very capacity of the interlocutors to present it. An extreme form of disagreement is where X cannot see the common object Y is presenting because X cannot comprehend that the sounds uttered by Y form words and chains of words similar to X's own. This extreme situation — first and foremost — concerns politics. Where philosophy encounters both politics and poetry at once, disagreement bears on what it means to be a being that uses words to argue. The structures proper to disagreement are those in which discussion of an argument comes down to a dispute over the object of the discussion and over the capacity of those who are making an object of it.

The following pages try to define a few pointers for understanding disagreement whereby the aporia of politics is embraced as a philosophical object. We will be testing the following hypothesis: that what is called "political philosophy" might well be the set of reflective operations whereby philosophy tries to rid itself of politics, to suppress a scandal in thinking proper to the exercise of politics. This theoretical scandal is nothing more than the rationality of disagreement. What makes politics an object of scandal is that it is that activity which has the rationality of disagreement as its very own rationality. The basis of philosophy's dispute with politics is thus the very reduction of the rationality of disagreement. This operation, whereby philosophy automatically expels disagreement from itself, is thereby identified with the project of "really" doing politics, of achieving the true essence of what politics talks about. Philosophy does not become "political" because politics is so crucial it simply must intervene. It becomes political because regulating the rationality situation of politics is a condition for defining what belongs to philosophy.

The book is organized along the following lines. It begins with the supposedly founding strands of thought in which Aristotle defines the logos proper to politics. It then attempts to reveal, in the determination of the logical-political animal, the point at which the logos splits, revealing what is *proper* to politics and which philosophy rejects with Plato and tries, with Aristotle, to appropriate. On the basis of Aristotle's text (and what this text stops short of), we will try to answer the question, what can be thought of specifically as politics? To think through this specificity will force us to distinguish it from what normally goes by the name of politics and for which I propose to reserve the term *policing*. On the basis of this distinction we will try to define first the logic of disagreement proper to political rationality, then the basis and major forms of "political philosophy" in the sense of a specific masking of this distinction. We will then try to think through the effect of the return of "political philosophy" in the field of political practice. This allows us to deduce a few landmarks for reflection that will clarify what might be understood by the term *democracy* and the way it differs from the practices and legitimizations of the consensus system, in order to appreciate what is practiced and said in the name of the end of politics or of its return, and what is exalted in the name of a humanity *sans frontières* and deplored in the name of the reign of the inhuman.

I must declare a double debt here: first to those who, by generously inviting me to speak on issues of politics, democracy, and justice have ended up persuading me I had something specific to say on the subject; and also to those with whom public, private, and occasionally mute dialogue has inspired me to try to define this specificity. They know what is their due in this anonymous thanks.

Chapter 1

The Beginning of Politics

Let's begin at the beginning, meaning the celebrated sentences in book I of Aristotle's *Politics* that define the eminently political nature of the human animal and lay the foundations of the city:

> Nature, as we say, does nothing without some purpose; and she has endowed man alone among the animals with the power of speech. Speech is something different from voice, which is possessed by other animals also and used by them to express pain or pleasure; for their nature does indeed enable them not only to feel pleasure and pain but to communicate these feelings to each other. Speech, on the other hand, serves to indicate what is useful and what is harmful, and so also what is just and what is unjust. For the real difference between man and other animals is that humans alone have perception of good and evil, the just and the unjust, etc. It is the sharing of a common view in these matters that makes a household and a state.[1]

The idea of the political nature of man is compressed into those few words: a chimera of the Ancients, according to Hobbes, who intended to replace it with an exact science of the motivating forces of human nature; or, conversely, the eternal principle of a politics of the common good and the education of the citizen, which Leo Strauss contrasts with the modern utilitarian tarting up of the demands of community. But before challenging or trumpeting such a notion of human nature, it might be an idea to come in a little earlier at the singularity of its deduction. The supremely political destiny of man is attested by a *sign:* the possession of the logos, that is, of speech, which *expresses,* while the voice simply *indicates.* What speech expresses, what it makes evident for a community of subjects who understand it, is the useful and the harmful and, consequently, the just and the unjust. The possession of such an organ of expression marks the separation between two kinds of animals as the difference between two modes of access to sense experience: that of pleasure and suffering, common to all animals endowed with a voice, and that of good and evil, exclusive to human beings and already present in the perception of the useful and the harmful. On this rests not the exclusivity of a bent for politics, politicity, but a politicity of a superior kind, which is achieved in the family and the city-state.

In this limpid demonstration several points remain obscure. No doubt any reader of Plato grasps that the objectivity of good is separate from the relativity of the pleasurable. But the division of their *aisthêsis* is not so obvious: where exactly do we draw the line between the unpleasant feeling of having received a blow and the feeling of having suffered an "injury" through this same blow? We could say that the difference is marked precisely in the logos that separates the discursive articulation of a grievance from the phonic articulation of a groan. But then the difference between unpleasantness and injury must be felt and felt as communicable, as defining a sphere of community of good and bad. The sign derived from the possession of the organ — articulated language — is one thing. The manner in which this organ exercises its function, in which language expresses a shared *aisthêsis,* is another. Teleological reasoning implies that the telos of common good is immanent to feeling and expression as the "injury" of pain inflicted by another person. But how exactly do we understand the logical connection between the "useful" and the "harmful" thus expressed and the strictly political order of justice? At first glance, the shameless utilitarian might remark to the noble partisan of the "classics" that this passage from the useful and the harmful to community justice is not so far removed from the utilitarian's own deduction of a common utility created by optimization of respective utilities and reduction of whatever is harmful. It seems hard to draw the line here between the community of Good and the utilitarian social contract.

Let's grant devotees of the "classics" this much: this line can and must be drawn. But it wends its way through some pretty dire straits where not only the so-called "utilitarian" denounced by Leo Strauss risks getting lost but also the person he himself shares with the utilitarians: whoever assimilates the logos expressing the just to that deliberation by which individuals' particularities are subsumed in the universality of the state. The problem here is not to ennoble acceptance of the useful to bring it up to par with the ideality of the just that is its goal; rather, it is being able to see that going from the useful to the just can only happen through mediation of their opposites. It is in the play of opposites, in the obscure relationship of the "harmful" and the "unjust," that the heart of the political problem lies — the problem politics poses for philosophical thinking about community. The connection between the useful and the just is indeed impeded by two heterogeneities. First, this is what separates such falsely opposed terms as "useful" and "harmful." Greek usage does not establish any clear opposition of the kind between Aristotle's terms *sumpheron* and *blaberon*. *Blaberon*, in fact, has two accepted meanings: in one sense it is the lot of unpleasantness that falls to an individual for whatever reason, whether it be through a natural catastrophe or human action, and in the other, it is the negative consequence that an individual suffers as a result of their action or, more often, the action of another. *Blabê* thus commonly connotes damage in the legal sense of the term, the objectively determinable wrong done by one individual to another. The notion normally therefore implies the idea of a relationship between two parties. *Sumpheron*, on the other hand, essentially designates a relationship to oneself, the advantage that an individual or a group gains or hopes to gain from an action. *Sum-*

pheron thus does not imply relationship to another, so the two terms are not genuine opposites. In general Greek usage what is usually contrasted to *blaberon* as wrong suffered is *ôphelimon,* the help one receives. In *The Nichomachean Ethics,* what Aristotle himself contrasts to *blaberon* as a bad lot is *aïreton,* the good lot to be derived. But the advantage, the *sumpheron,* that one individual receives is in no way the correlative of an equivalent disadvantage suffered by another. For Thrasymachus such a correlation exists, for this is the false conclusion he reaches in book I of the *Republic,* when he translates into terms of profit and loss his enigmatic and polysemic formula: justice is the advantage of the superior man *(to sumpheron tou kreittonos).* For Thrasymachus the profit of the shepherd is the loss of the sheep, the advantage of the governors the disadvantage of the governed, and so on. We might add in passing that to translate this concept as it is usually translated as "the interest of the strongest" is to immediately get locked into the position Plato locks Thrasymachus in; it is to short-circuit Plato's entire demonstration, which plays on the polysemy of the formula to bring off a double disjunction. Not only is the "profit" of one not the "loss" of another but, moreover, superiority strictly speaking only ever has one beneficiary: the "inferior" over whom it exercises dominion. In this demonstration, one term disappears — wrong. What Thrasymachus's refutation anticipates is a city without wrong, a city in which the superiority exercised according to the natural order produces a reciprocity of services between the guardian protectors and the artisans who provide for them.

Therein lies the second problem and the second heterogeneity. For Plato, as for Aristotle, who is on this score faithful to his master, the just city is basically a state in which the *sumpheron* has no correlative *blaberon.* Proper distribution of "advantages" presupposes prior elimination of a certain wrong, of a certain regime of wrong. "What wrong have you done me, what wrong have I done you?" According to the *Theaetetus,* this is how the advocate talks as an expert in transactions and tribunals — in other words, as a person absolutely ignorant of the justice that is the basis of the city. Such justice only begins wherever uses stop being parceled out, wherever profits and losses stop being

4

weighed. Justice as the basis of community has not yet come into play wherever the sole concern is with preventing individuals who live together from doing each other reciprocal wrongs and with reestablishing the balance of profits and losses whenever they do so. It only begins when what is at issue is what citizens have *in common* and when the main concern is with the way the forms of exercising and of controlling the exercising of this common capacity are divided up. On the one hand, justice as virtue is not a simple balancing act of individual interests or reparation of the damage done by some to others. It is the choice of the very measuring rod by which each party takes only what is its due. On the other hand, political justice is not simply the order that holds measured relationships between individuals and goods together. It is the order that determines the partition of what is common. Now, in this order, the just cannot be deduced from the useful as in the order of individuals. For individuals, the problem of going from the order of the useful to the order of the just can easily be resolved. Book V of *The Nichomachean Ethics* offers a solution to our problem: justice consists in not taking more than one's share of advantageous things or less than one's share of disadvantageous things. On condition of reducing *bla-beron* to the "harmful" and of identifying *sumpheron* with these "advantageous" things, it is possible to give a precise meaning to the passage from the order of the useful to that of the just: the advantageous and the disadvantageous are the matter over which the virtue of justice is exercised, the latter consisting in taking the appropriate share, the average share of each and every one.

The problem, obviously, is that this still does not define any political order. The political begins precisely when one stops balancing profits and losses and worries instead about distributing *common* lots and evening out communal shares and entitlements to these shares, the *axiaï* entitling one to community. For the political community to be more than a contract between those exchanging goods and services, the reigning equality needs to be radically different from that according to which merchandise is exchanged and wrongs redressed. But the "classics" buff would be a bit rash to leap in and see in this the superiority of the common good, whose telos is contained in human nature, over the haggling on behalf of individual interests. The root of the problem lies here: for the founders of "political philosophy," this submission of the logic of exchange to the common good is expressed in a perfectly determined way, as the submission of arithmetical equality, which presides over commercial exchanges and over juridical sentences, to that geometric equality responsible for proportion, for common harmony, submission of the shares of the common held by each party in the community to the share that party brings to the common good. But this shift from vulgar arithmetic to an ideal geometry itself implies a curious compromise with the empirical, an odd way of counting the "parties" within the community. For the city to be ordered according to the good, community shares must be strictly in proportion to the *axia* of each part of the community: to the *value* it brings to the community and to the *right* that this value bestows on it to hold a share of the common power. Behind the problematic opposition between *sumpheron* and *blaberon* the essential political question lies. For political philosophy to exist, the order of political idealities must be linked to some construction of city "parts," to a count whose complexities may mask a fundamental miscount, a miscount that may well be the *blaberon*, the very wrong that is the stuff of politics. What the "classics" teach us first and foremost is that politics is not a matter of ties between individuals or of relationships between individuals and the community. Politics arises from a count of community "parts," which is always a false count, a double count, or a miscount.

Let's take a closer look at these *axiaï*. Aristotle sees three: the wealth of the smallest number *(oligoï)*, the virtue or excellence *(aretê)* from which the best *(aristoï)* derive their name, and the freedom *(eleutheria)* that belongs to the people *(demos)*. Taken on their own, each of these attributes yields a particular regime, threatened by the sedition of the others: the oligarchy of the rich, the aristocracy of the good, or the democracy of the people. On the other hand, the precise combination of their community entitlements procures the common good. But a secret imbalance spoils this pretty picture. Doubtless one can measure the respective contribution of oligarchs and aristocrats and the control of the people in the quest for the common good. Book III of *Politics* attempts to make this calculation concrete, to define the measure of political capacity held respectively by the minority of men of "merit" and by the majority of ordinary men. The metaphor of mixing allows Aristotle to imagine a community nourished by the proportional addition of respective qualities "in something like the way," he tells us, "that a combination of coarse foods with refined renders the whole diet more nutritious than a small amount of the latter."[2] The pure and the impure are able to blend their effects. But how can they basically be compared with each other? What exactly is the entitlement or quality of each party? Within the beautiful harmony of the *axiaï*, one single easily recognizable quality stands out: the wealth of the *oligoï*. Yet this is also the one quality that derives exclusively from the arithmetic of exchange. So what does the freedom of the people bring to the community? And in what is it peculiar to them? This is where the fundamental miscount rears its head. First, the freedom of the demos is not a determinable property but a pure invention: behind "autochthony," the myth of origins revindicated by the demos of Athens, the brute fact that makes democracy a scandalous theoretical object impinges. Simply by being born in a certain city, and more especially in the city of Athens once enslavement for debt was abolished there, any one of these speaking bodies doomed to the anonymity of work and of reproduction, these speaking bodies that are of no more value than slaves — even less, says Aristotle, since the slave gets his virtue from the virtue of his master — any old artisan or shopkeeper whatsoever is counted in this party to the city that calls itself the people, as taking part in community affairs as such. The simple impossibility of the *oligoï*'s reducing their debtors to slavery was transformed into the appearance of a freedom that was to be the positive property of the people as a part of the community.

There are those who attribute this promotion of the people and their freedom to the wisdom of the good legislator, Solon providing the archetype. Others refer to the "demagogy" of certain nobles who turned the populace into a bastion against their rivals. Each of these explanations already supposes a certain idea of politics. Rather than opt for one or the other, it would be better to pause to consider what lies behind them: the original nexus of fact and law and the peculiar connection this nexus established between two key terms in politics, equality and liberty. "Liberal" wisdom smugly tells us of the perverse effects of an artificial equality that came along and blocked the natural freedom of enterprise and exchange. The classic authors, however, encounter a phenomenon of a very different profundity at the beginnings of politics: it is freedom, as an empty property, that came along and set a limit on the calculations of commercial equality and the effects of the simple law of *owing* and *having*. Freedom, in sum, pops up and splits the oligarchy, preventing it from governing through the simple arithmetical play of profits and debts. The law of the oligarchy is effectively that "arithmetical" equality should command without hindrance, that wealth should be immediately identical with domination. One might think that the poor of Athens were subject to the power of the nobles rather than that of the merchants, but the point is that the liberty of the people of Athens reduced the natural domination of the nobility, based on the illustrious and ancient nature of their lineage, to their simple domination as wealthy property owners and monopolizers of the common property. It reduced the nobility to their condition as the rich and transformed their absolute right, reduced to the power of the rich, into a particular *axia.*

But the miscount does not stop there. Not only does freedom as what is "proper" to the demos not allow itself to be determined by any positive property; it is not proper to the demos at all. The people are nothing more than the undifferentiated mass of those who have no positive qualification — no wealth, no virtue — but who are nonetheless acknowledged to enjoy the same freedom as those who do. The people who make up the people are in fact simply free *like* the rest. Now it is this simple identity with those who are otherwise superior to them in all things that gives them a specific qualification. The demos attributes to itself as its proper lot the equality that belongs to all citizens. In so doing, this party that is not one identifies its improper property with the exclusive principle of community and identifies its name — the name of the indistinct mass of men of no position — with the name of the community itself. For freedom — which is merely the position of those who have absolutely no other, no merit, no wealth — is counted at the same time as being common virtue. It allows the demos (that is, the actual gathering of men of no position, these men whom Aristotle tells us "had no part in anything"[3]) to identify with the whole of the community through homonymy. This is the fundamental wrong, the original nexus of *blaberon* and *adikon* whose "manifestation" then blocks any deduction of the just from the useful: the people appropriate the common quality as their own. What they bring to the community strictly speaking is contention. This should be understood in a double sense: the qualification that the people bring is a contentious property since it does not belong exclusively to the people, but this contentious property is strictly speaking only the setting-up of a contentious commonality. The mass of men without qualities identify with the community in the name of the wrong that is constantly being done to them by those whose position or qualities have the natural effect of propelling them into the nonexistence of those who have "no part in anything." It is in the name of the wrong done them by the other parties that the people identify with the whole of the community. Whoever has no part — the poor of ancient times, the third estate, the modern proletariat — cannot in fact have any part other than all or nothing. On top of this, it is through the existence of this part of those who have no part, of this nothing that is all, that the community exists as a political community — that is, as divided by a fundamental dispute, by a dispute to do with the counting of the community's parts even more than of their "rights." The people are not one class among others. They are the class of the wrong that harms the community and establishes it as a "community" of the just and the unjust.

So it is that scandalizing men of substance, the demos, that horde who have nothing, become the people, the political community of free Athenians, the community that speaks, is counted, and deliberates at the assembly, causing wordsmiths to write, Ἔδοξε τῷ Δήμῳ: "it has pleased the people, the people have decided." For Plato, the man who invented political philosophy for us, this formula easily translates into the equivalence of two terms: demos and doxa: it has pleased those who know only those illusions of more or less that are called pleasure and pain; there was simple doxa, "appearance" for the people, appearance of the people. The people are the mere appearance produced by the sensations of pleasure and pain manipulated by rhetoricians and sophists to stroke or intimidate the great animal, the morass of folk who have nothing, gathered together at the assembly.

Let's be clear at the outset: in his resolute hatred of democracy, Plato delves much further into the foundations of politics and democracy than those tired apologists who assure us lukewarmly that we should love democracy "reasonably," meaning "moderately." Plato sees what they have overlooked: democracy's miscount, which is, after all, merely the fundamental miscount of politics. There is politics—and not just domination—because there is a wrong count of the parts of the whole. This impossible equation is resumed in a formula Herodotus lends to Otanes, the Persian: ἐν γὰρ τῷ πολλῷ ἔνι τὰ πάντα, the whole lies in the many.[4] The demos is that many that is identical to the whole: the many as one, the part as the whole, the all in all. The nonexistent qualitative difference of freedom produces this impossible equation that cannot be understood within the divisions of arithmetical equality, requiring the compensation of profits and losses, or of geometric equality, which is supposed to link a quality to a rank. By the same token, the people are always more or less than the people. The well-born and comfortably placed may laugh or cry over all the signs of what looks to them like fraud or usurpation: the demos means the majority and not the assembly, the assembly and not the community, the poor in the name of the city, clapping their agreement, counting stones instead of taking decisions. But all these manifestations of the people's being unequal to themselves are just the small beer of a basic miscount: that impossible equality of the multiple and the whole produced by appropriation of freedom as being peculiar to the people. This impossible equality has a domino effect on the entire deduction of shares and entitlements that make up the city. Following from this singular property of the demos, it is virtue, the property of the *aristoï,* that emerges as the space of a curious ambiguity. Who exactly are these men of substance or these excellent ones bringing virtue to the communal pot the way the people bring a freedom that is not theirs to bring? If they are not the philosopher's dream, the count of his dream of proportion converted into a part of the whole, they may well be merely another name for the *oligoï*—in other words, quite simply, the rich. Even Aristotle, who is at pains in *The Nichomachean Ethics* and book III of *Politics* to give substance to the three parts and the three ranks, freely admits in book IV and also in *The Athenian Constitution* that the city actually has only two parties, the rich and the poor: "almost everywhere the wellborn and the welloff are coextensive."[5] The arrangements that distribute powers or the appearances of power between these two parties alone, these irreducible parts of the city, are required to bring off that community *aretê* that the *aristoï* will always be lacking.

Are we to understand by this simply that the scientific counts of geometric proportion are merely ideal constructions by which philosophy in its good will originally seeks to correct the essential, inescapable reality of class struggle? This question can only be answered in two parts. It must first be emphasized that the Ancients, much more than the Moderns, acknowledged that the whole basis of politics is the struggle between the poor and the rich. But that's just it: what they acknowledged was a strictly political reality—even if it meant trying to overcome it. The struggle between the rich and the poor is not social reality, which politics then has to deal with. It is the actual institution of politics itself. There is politics when there is a part of those who have no part, a part or party of the poor. Politics does not happen just because the poor oppose the rich. It is the other way around: politics (that is, the interruption of the simple effects of domination by the rich) causes the poor to exist as an entity. The outrageous claim of the demos to be the whole of the community only satisfies in its own way—that of a *party*—the requirement of politics. Politics exists when the natural order of domination is interrupted by the institution of a part of those who have no part. This institution is the whole of politics as a specific form of connection. It defines the common of the community as a political community, in other words, as divided, as based on a wrong that escapes the arithmetic of exchange and reparation. Beyond this set-up there is no politics. There is only the order of domination or the disorder of revolt.

Herodotus serves up this simple alternative in a tale that takes the form of an apologia. This exemplary history-apologia is devoted to the revolt of the Scythian slaves. The Scythians, he tells us, customarily put out the eyes of those they reduced to slavery, the better to restrict them to their task as slaves, which was to milk the livestock. This normal order of things was disturbed by the Scythians' great expeditions. Having left to conquer Media, the Scythian warriors plunged deep into Asia and were held up there for a whole generation. Over the same period, a generation of sons was born to the slaves and raised with their eyes open. Looking around at the world, they reached the conclusion that there was no particular reason why they should be slaves, being born the same way their distant masters were and with the same attributes. Since the women who remained behind permanently took it upon themselves to confirm this natural similarity, the slaves decided that, until proved wrong, they were the equal of the warriors. They consequently surrounded the territory with a great big trench and armed themselves, ready to hold their ground when the conquerors should return. When the latter finally showed up with their lances and bows, they thought they could easily clean up this little cowherds' revolt. The assault was a failure. One of the sharper warriors took the measure of the situation and summed it up for his brothers in arms:

> "Take my advice—lay spear and bow aside, and let each man fetch his horsewhip, and go boldly up to them. So long as they see us with arms in our hands, they imagine themselves our equals in birth and bravery; but let them behold us with no other weapon but the whip, and they will feel that they are our slaves, and flee before us."[6]

And so it was done, with great success: struck by the spectacle, the slaves took to their heels without a fight.

Herodotus's tale helps us to see how the paradigm of the "slave war" and the "rebel slave" became the other side of any manifestation of the struggle between the "poor" and the "rich." The paradigm of the slave war is one of a purely war-generated achievement of equality between the dominated and the dominator. The Scythian slaves occupy the territory of their former servitude as a fortified camp and oppose arms with arms. This egalitarian demonstration at first throws those who thought they were their natural masters. But when the latter once more show the signs of their difference in nature, the rebels have no comeback. What they cannot do is transform equality in war into political freedom. This equality, literally mapped out over the territory and defended by force of arms, does not create a divided community. It cannot be transformed into the improper property of that freedom that establishes the demos simultaneously as both part of and as the whole of the community. Now, politics comes about solely through interruption, the initial twist that institutes politics as the deployment of a wrong or of a fundamental dispute. This twist is the wrong, the fundamental *blaberon* that philosophical theorizing about community runs up against. *Blaberon* signifies "that which stops the current," according to one of the invented etymologies in *Cratylus*,[7] which wouldn't be the first time such invented etymologies touched on an essential crux of thought. *Blaberon* signifies an interrupted current, the original twist that short-circuits the natural logic of "properties." This interruption obliges one to think about proportion, the *analogia* of the community body. It also spoils in advance the dream of such proportion.

For the wrong is not just the class struggle, internal dissension to be overcome by giving the city its principle of unity, by founding the city on the *arkhê*—starting point or basis—of community. It is the very impossibility of *arkhê*. It would be too easy if there were just the calamity of the struggle between rich and poor. The solution to the problem would have been found pretty quickly. All you have to do is get rid of the cause of dissension, in other words, the inequality of wealth, by giving each an equal share of the cake. The trouble runs deeper. Just as the people are not really the people but actually the poor, the poor themselves are not really the poor. They are merely the reign of a lack of position, the effectivity of the initial disjunction that bears the empty name of freedom, the improper property, entitlement to dispute. They are themselves in advance the warped conjunction of what is proper to them that is not really proper to them and of the common that is not really common. They are simply the constitutive wrong or torsion of politics as such. The party of the poor embodies nothing other than politics itself as the setting-up of a part of those who have no part. Symmetrically, the party of the rich embodies nothing other than the antipolitical. From Athens in the fifth century B.C. up until our own governments, the party of the rich has only ever said one thing, which is most precisely the negation of politics: there is no part of those who have no part.

This fundamental proposition may of course be inflected in different ways according to what is known as the evolution of moral values and attitudes. In the old forthright tone of the Ancients that persists among "liberals" of the nineteenth century, it goes like this: there are only chiefs and indians, those of substance and those of no account, elites and unwashed masses, experts and ignorant fools. In contemporary euphemism, the proposition is put differently: there are only *parts* of society — social majorities and minorities, socioprofessional categories, interest groups, communities, and so on. There are only parts that must be converted into partners. But under the policed forms of contractual society and of government by consultation, as in the stark forms of nonegalitarian affirmative action, the fundamental proposition remains the same: there is no part of those who have no part. There are only the parts of parties. In other words, there is no politics, nor should there be. The war of the poor and the rich is also a war over the very existence of politics. The dispute over the count of the poor as the people, and of the people as the community, is a dispute about the existence of politics through which politics occurs. Politics is the sphere of activity of a common that can only ever be contentious, the relationship between parts that are only parties and credentials or entitlements whose sum never equals the whole.

This is the initial scandal of politics that the facts of democracy invite philosophy to ponder. Philosophy's atomic project, as summed up in Plato, is to replace the arithmetical order, the order of more or less that regulates the exchange of perishable goods and human woes, with the divine order of geometric proportion that regulates the real good, the common good that is virtually each person's advantage without being to anyone's disadvantage. For this, a science, the science of mathematics, will provide the model, the model of an order of numbering whose very rigor derives from the fact that it escapes the common measure. The path of good lies in substituting a mathematics of the incommensurable for the arithmetic of shopkeepers and barterers. The only hitch is that there is at least one sphere in which the simple order of more or less has been left hanging, replaced by a specific order, a specific proportion. This sphere is called politics. Politics exists through the fact of a magnitude that escapes ordinary measurement, this part of those who have no part that is nothing and everything. This paradoxical magnitude has already pulled the plug on market measures, stopped the "current," suspended the effects of arithmetic on the social body. In the city and in the soul, as in the science of surfaces, volumes, and stars, philosophy strives to replace arithmetical equality with geometric equality. But what the empty freedom of the Athenians presents philosophy with is the effect of another kind of equality, one that suspends simple arithmetic without setting up any kind of geometry. This equality is simply the equality of anyone at all with anyone else: in other words, in the final analysis, the absence of *arkhê,* the sheer contingency of any social order. The author of the *Gorgias* pours all his scorn into proving that this particular equality is nothing more than the arithmetical equality of the oligarchs, in other words, the inequality of desire, the boundless appetite that makes vulgar souls go round in a vicious circle of pleasure endlessly accompanied by pain and that makes regimes go round in the vicious circle of oligarchies, democracies, and tyrannies. The "equality" that the leaders of the popular party have bestowed on the people of Athens is no more to them than an endless craving for the always more: always more ports and ships, more merchandise and colonies, arsenals and fortifications. But Plato knows full well that the problem lies deeper. The problem is not this insatiable hunger for ships and fortifications. It is that at the people's assembly, any mere shoemaker or smithie can get up and have his say on how to steer the ships and how to build the fortifications and, more to the point, on the just or unjust way to use these for the common good. The problem is not the *always more* but the *anyone at all*, the sudden revelation of the ultimate *anarchy* on which any hierarchy rests. The debate about nature versus convention that pits Socrates against Protagoras or Callicles remains a reassuring way of presenting the scandal. The foundation of politics is not in fact more a matter of convention than of nature: it is the lack of foundation, the sheer contingency of any social order. Politics exists simply because no social order is based on nature, no divine law regulates human society. This is the lesson Plato himself offers in the great myth of *Politics*. It is pointless to try to look for models in the age of Khronos and the inane reveries of the shepherd kings. Between the age of Khronos and ourselves, the disconnection of wrong has already happened. Whenever someone thinks about establishing the theoretical rules of a city's proportions, it means that democracy has already passed that way. Our world goes round "the other way," and anyone who wants to cure politics of its ills has only one available solution: the lie that invents some kind of social nature in order to provide the community with an *arkhê*.

Politics occurs because, or when, the natural order of the shepherd kings, the warlords, or property owners is interrupted by a freedom that crops up and makes real the ultimate equality on which any social order rests. Before the logos that deals with the useful and the harmful, there is the logos that orders and bestows the right to order. But this initial logos is tainted with a primary contradiction. There is order in society because some people command and others obey, but in order to obey an order at least two things are required: you must understand the order and you must understand that you must obey it. And to do that, you must already be the equal of the person who is ordering you. It is this equality that gnaws away at any natural order. Doubtless infe-

riors obey 99 percent of the time; it remains that the social order is reduced thereby to its ultimate contingency. In the final analysis, inequality is only possible through equality. This means that politics doesn't
always happen—it actually happens very little or rarely. What is usually
lumped together under the name of political history or political science
in fact stems more often than not from other mechanisms concerned
with holding on to the exercise of majesty, the curacy of divinity, the
command of armies, and the management of interests. Politics only
occurs when these mechanisms are stopped in their tracks by the effect
of a presupposition that is totally foreign to them yet without which
none of them could ultimately function: the presupposition of the equality of anyone and everyone, or the paradoxical effectiveness of the sheer
contingency of any order.

This ultimate secret of politics was expressed by a "Modern," Thomas
Hobbes, who took the risk of rebaptizing it, for the purposes of his
cause, "the war of all against all." The "Ancients" circle in on this equality quite precisely while avoiding naming it, because freedom for them
was defined in relation to a most specific contrary, slavery. The slave is
the one who has the capacity to understand a logos without having
the capacity of the logos. He is the specific transition from animality
to humanity that Aristotle defines most precisely as participating in
the linguistic community by way of comprehension but not understanding: ὁ κοινωνῶν λόγου τοσοῦτον ὅσον αἰσθάνεσθαι ἀλλὰ μὴ
ἔχειν·, the slave is the one who participates in reason so far as to recognize it *(aisthêsis)* but not so as to possess it *(hexis)*.[8] The contingent
naturalness of the freedom of the man of the people and the naturalness of slavery can then be distinguished without referring back to the
ultimate contingency of equality. This is also to say that such equality
can be posited as having no bearing on something like politics. It is
the demonstration that Plato had already performed by having Menon's
slave discover the rule of the square root. That an insignificant slave
can arrive as well as Socrates at an operation separating the geometric
from the arithmetical order, that he might share in the same intelligence,
does not define for him any form of inclusion in the community.

The "classics" clearly home in on the original equality of the logos without naming it. Yet what they do define, and in a way that remains incomprehensible to modern theorists of the social contract and life in the state of nature, is the torsion that this principle that is not one creates, when it takes effect as the "freedom" of people who have nothing. Politics occurs when the egalitarian contingency disrupts the natural pecking order as the "freedom" of the people, when this disruption produces a specific mechanism: the dividing of society into parts that are not "true" parts; the setting-up of one part as equal to the whole in the name of a "property" that is not its own, and of a "common" that is the community of a dispute. This is ultimately that wrong that slips in between the useful and the just and rules out any deducing of one from the other. The setting-up of politics is identical to the institution of the class struggle. The class struggle is not the secret motor of politics or the hidden truth behind appearances. It is politics itself, politics such as it is encountered, always in place already, by whoever tries to found the community on its *arkhê*. This is not to say that politics exists because social groups have entered into battle over their divergent interests. The torsion or twist that causes politics to occur is also what establishes each class as being different from itself. The proletariat is not so much a class as the dissolution of all classes; this is what constitutes its universality, as Marx would say. The claim should be understood in all its generality. Politics is the setting-up of a dispute between classes that are not really classes. "True" classes are, or should be, real parts of society, categories that correspond to functions. This is not the case with the Athenian demos, which identifies with the entire community, or with the Marxist proletariat, which declares itself to be the radical exception to the community. Both bring together, in the name of one part of society, the sheer name of equality between anyone and everyone by means of which all classes disconnect and politics occurs. The universality of politics is that of each party's difference from itself as well as of the differend as the very structure of community. The wrong instituted by politics is not primarily class warfare; it is the difference of each class from itself, which then imposes on the very carving up of the social

18

body the law of mixing, the law of anyone at all doing anything at all. Plato has a word for this: *polupragmosunê*, the fact of going on "a bit," of going "a bit too far," of anyone finding themselves performing any function whatever. If the *Gorgias* is an interminable demonstration that democratic equality is just the inequality of tyranny, the *Republic* goes about endlessly tracking down this *polupragmosunê*, this confusion of activities, fit to destroy any ordered allocation of state functions and to cause the different classes to lose their proper character. Book IV of the *Republic,* at the point where it defines justice — true justice, that which excludes wrong — solemnly warns us that such confusion "does the greatest harm to our state, and we are entirely justified in calling it the worst of evils."[9]

Politics begins with a major wrong: the gap created by the empty freedom of the people between the arithmetical order and the geometric order. It is not common usefulness that founds the political community any more than confrontation or the forming of interests. The wrong by which politics occurs is not some flaw calling for reparation. It is the introduction of an incommensurable at the heart of the distribution of speaking bodies. This incommensurable breaks not only with the equality of profits and losses; it also ruins in advance the project of the city ordered according to the proportion of the *cosmos* and based on the *arkhê* of the community.

Chapter 2

Wrong: Politics and Police

The brilliant deduction of the political animal's ends from the properties of the logical animal patches over a tear. Between the useful and the just lies the incommensurability of wrong, which alone establishes the body politic as antagonism between parts of the community that are not real parts of the social body. But in turn the false continuity between the useful and the just points up the falseness of evidence of any decisive opposition between human beings endowed with the logos and animals restricted to sole use of the organ of the voice *(phônê)*. The voice, Aristotle tells us, is an organ designed for a limited purpose. It serves animals in general to indicate or show *(sêmainein)* sensations of pain or pleasure. Pleasure and pain exist outside the distribution that reserves for human beings and the body politic a sense of the profitable and the injurious, *and so* the placing in common of the just and the unjust. But, in distributing so clearly the ordinary functions of the voice and the privileges of speech, surely Aristotle has not forgotten the furious accusations leveled by his master, Plato, at that "large and powerful animal," the people? Book VI of the *Republic* actually takes pleasure in showing us the large and powerful animal responding to words that soothe it with a roar of cheers and to those that annoy it with a disapproving racket. The "science" of those animal tamers in charge of it who show themselves within the walls of its pen consists entirely in knowing what vocal effects make the great animal growl and those that make it nice and gentle. Just as the demos usurps entitlement to community, democracy is the regime — the way of life — in which the voice, which not only expresses but also procures the illusory feelings of pleasure and pain, usurps the privileges of the logos, which allows the just to be recognized and organizes this realization in terms of community proportion. The metaphor of the large and powerful animal is no simple metaphor: it serves to rigorously reject as animals those speaking beings with no position who introduce trouble into the logos and into its political realization as *analogia* of the parts of the community.

So the simple opposition between logical animals and phonic animals is in no way the given on which politics is then based. It is, on the contrary, one of the stakes of the very dispute that institutes politics. At the heart of politics lies a double wrong, a fundamental conflict, never conducted as such, over the relationship between the capacity of the speaking being who is without qualification and political capacity. For Plato, the mob of anonymous speaking beings who call themselves the people does wrong to any organized distribution of bodies in community. But conversely, "the people" is the name, the form of subjectification, of this immemorial and perennial wrong through which the social order is symbolized by dooming the majority of speaking beings to the night of silence or to the animal noise of voices expressing pleasure or pain. For before the debts that place people who are of no account in a relationship of dependence on the oligarchs, there is the symbolic distribution of bodies that divides them into two categories: those that one sees and those that one does not see, those who have a logos — memorial speech, an account to be kept up — and those who have no logos, those who really speak and those whose voice merely mimics the articulate voice to express pleasure and pain. Politics exists because the logos is never simply speech, because it is always indissolubly the *account* that

22

is made of this speech: the account by which a sonorous emission is understood as speech, capable of enunciating what is just, whereas some other emission is merely perceived as a noise signaling pleasure or pain, consent or revolt.

This is what a nineteenth-century French thinker tells us in his rewriting of the tale told by Livy of the secession of the Roman plebeians on Aventine Hill. From 1829, in the *Revue de Paris,* Pierre-Simon Ballanche published a series of articles under the heading "Formule générale de l'histoire de tous les peuples appliquée à l'histoire du peuple romain" (General formula of the history of all peoples applied to the history of the Roman people). In his own way Ballanche thereby makes the connection between the politics of the "Ancients" and that of the "Moderns." Livy's tale links up the end of the war with the Volscians, the retreat of the plebs over Aventine Hill, the ambassadorship of Menenius Agrippa, his famous fable [of the revolt of the body's members, in which the body is a metaphor of the social body], and the return of the plebs to order. Ballanche reproaches the Latin historian for being unable to think of the event as anything other than a revolt, an uprising caused by poverty and anger and sparking a power play devoid of all meaning. Livy is incapable of supplying the meaning of the conflict because he is incapable of locating Menenius Agrippa's fable in its real context: that of a quarrel over the issue of speech itself. By centering his story-apologia on the discussions of the senators and the speech acts of the plebs, Ballanche performs a restaging of the conflict in which the entire issue at stake involves finding out whether there exists a common stage where plebeians and patricians can debate anything.

The position of the intransigent patricians is straightforward: there is no place for discussion with the plebs for the simple reason that plebs do not speak. They do not speak because they are beings without a name, deprived of logos — meaning, of symbolic enrollment in the city. Plebs live a purely individual life that passes on nothing to posterity except for life itself, reduced to its reproductive function. Whoever is nameless *cannot* speak. Consul Menenius made a fatal mistake in imagining that *words* were issuing from the mouths of the plebs when logically the only thing that could issue forth was noise.

> "They have speech like us, they dared tell Menenius! Was it a god
> that shut Menenius's mouth, that dazzled his eyes, that made his
> ears ring? Did some holy daze take hold of him? . . . He was some-
> how unable to respond that they had only transitory speech, a
> speech that is a fugitive sound, a sort of lowing, a sign of want
> and not an expression of intelligence. They were deprived of the
> eternal word which was in the past and would be in the future."[1]

This discourse that Ballanche attributes to Appius Claudius sets out perfectly the terms of the quarrel. Between the language of those who have a name and the lowing of nameless beings, no situation of linguistic exchange can possibly be set up, no rules or code of discussion. This verdict does not simply reflect the obstinacy of the dominant or their ideological blindness; it strictly expresses the sensory order that organizes their domination, which is that domination itself. Before becoming a class traitor, the consul Menenius, who imagines he has heard the plebs speak, is a victim of sensory illusion. The order that structures patrician domination recognizes no logos capable of being articulated by beings deprived of logos, no *speech* capable of being proffered by nameless beings, beings of no *ac/count*.

Faced with this, what do the plebs gathered on the Aventine do? They do not set up a fortified camp in the manner of the Scythian slaves. They do what would have been unthinkable for the latter: they establish another order, another partition of the perceptible, by constituting themselves not as warriors equal to other warriors but as speaking beings sharing the same properties as those who deny them these. They thereby execute a series of speech acts that mimic those of the patricians: they pronounce imprecations and apotheoses; they delegate one of their number to go and consult *their* oracles; they give themselves representatives by rebaptizing them. In a word, they conduct themselves like beings with names. Through transgression, they find that they too, just like speaking beings, are endowed with speech that does not simply express want, suffering, or rage, but intelligence. They write, Ballanche tells us, "a name in the sky": a place in the symbolic order of the community of speaking beings, in a community that does not yet have any effective power in the city of Rome.

The story presents us with these two scenes and shows us the two observers and emissaries moving about between them — in only one direction, of course. These are atypical patricians who have come to see and hear what is going on in this staging of a nonexistent right. And they observe this incredible phenomenon: the plebeians have actually violated the order of the city. They have given themselves names. They have carried out a series of speech acts linking the life of their bodies to words and word use. In short, in Ballanche's terms, from being "mortals," they have become "men," that is, beings engaging in a collective destiny through words. They have become beings who may very well make promises and draw up contracts. The result is that, when Menenius delivers his apologia, they listen politely and thank him but only so they can then ask him for a treaty. He can cry out and say such a thing is impossible; unfortunately, Ballanche tells us, his apologia had, in a single day, "aged a whole cycle." It is easy to formulate the position: from the moment the plebs could understand Menenius's apologia — the apologia of the necessary inequality between the vital patrician principle and the plebeian members carrying it out — they were already, just as necessarily, equals. The apologia implies an inegalitarian partition of the perceptible. The sense necessary to understand this division presupposes an egalitarian division that puts paid to the former, but only the deployment of a specific scene of revelation gives this equality any effectiveness. Only such a mechanism can gauge the distance between the logos and itself or make this measurement effective in organizing a sensory space where plebeians happen to speak *like* patricians and the latter's domination has no basis other than the sheer contingency of any social order.

The Roman Senate of Ballanche's tale is animated by a secret council of wise old men. They know that when a cycle is over, it is over, whether you like it or not, and they conclude that, since the plebs have become creatures of speech, there is nothing left to do but to talk to them. This conclusion is in keeping with the philosophy that Ballanche derives from Vico: passing from one age of speech to another is not a matter of a rebellion that can be put down; it is a question of some kind of progressive revelation that can be recognized by its own signs and against which there is no point fighting.

What matters to us here, though, more than this determined philosophy, is the manner in which the apologia homes in on the relationship between the privilege of the logos and the litigious play that sets up the political stage. Before the gauging of interests and entitlements to this or that share, the dispute concerns the existence of parties as parties and the existence of a relationship that constitutes them as such. The double sense of logos, as speech and as account, is the space where this conflict is played out. The Aventine apologia allows us to reformulate Aristotle's pronouncement about the political function of the human logos and the significance of the wrong it makes manifest. The speech that causes politics to exist is the same that gauges the very gap between speech and the account of it. And the *aisthêsis* that shows itself in this speech is the very quarrel over the constitution of the *aisthêsis*, over this partition of the perceptible through which bodies find themselves in community. This division should be understood here in the double sense of the term: as community and as separation. It is the relationship between these that defines a division of the perceptible, and it is this relationship that is at play in the "double sense" of the apologia: the sense it implies and the sense required to understand it. To find out if plebs can speak is to find out if there is anything "between" the parties. For the patricians, there is no political stage *because* there are no parties. There are no parties because the plebeians, having no logos, *are not.* "Your misfortune is not to be," a patrician tells the plebs, "and this misfortune is inescapable."[2] This is the decisive point obscurely indicated by Aristotelian definition or Platonic polemics, but plainly eclipsed, on the other hand, by all the political community's notions of trade, contracts, and communication. Politics is primarily conflict over the existence of a common stage and over the existence and status of those present on it. It must first be established that the stage exists for the use of an interlocutor who can't see it and who can't see it for good reason *because* it doesn't exist. Parties do not exist prior to the conflict they name and in which they are counted as parties. The "discussion" of wrong is not an exchange—not even a violent one—between constituent partners. It concerns the speech situation itself and its performers. Politics does not exist because men, through the privilege of speech, place their interests in common. Politics exists because those who have no right to be counted as speaking beings make themselves of some account, setting up a community by the fact of placing in common a wrong that is nothing more than this very confrontation, the contradiction of two worlds in a single world: the world where they are and the world where they are not, the world where there is something "between" them and those who do not acknowledge them as speaking beings who count and the world where there is nothing.

The contingent, factitious nature of Athenian freedom and the exceptional nature of the "Secession of the Plebs" thus stage a fundamental conflict that is at once marked and missed by the slave war of Scythia. This conflict separates two modes of human being-together, two types of partition of the perceptible that are opposed in principle and yet bound up together in the impossible counts of proportion, as well as in the violence of conflict. There is the mode of being-together that puts bodies in their place and their role according to their "properties," according to their name or their lack of a name, the "logical" or "phonic" nature of the sounds that come out of their mouths. The principle of this kind of being-together is simple: it gives to each the part that is his due according to the evidence of what he is. Ways of being, ways of doing, and ways of saying—or not saying—precisely reflect each person's due. The Scythians, in putting out the eyes of those who need only their hands to carry out the task the Scythians demand they perform, offer the most primitive example. Patricians who can't understand the speech of those who can't possibly have any offer the classic case. The "politics" of communications and the opinion poll, which offer each of us, day and night, the endless spectacle of a world that has become indifferent and an exact count of what each age bracket or each socio-professional category thinks of the "political future" of this or that minister, could well be an exemplary modern form of the same thing. On the one hand, there is the logic that simply counts the lots of the parties, that distributes bodies within the space of their visibility or their invisibility and aligns ways of being, ways of doing, and ways of saying appropriate to each. And there is the other logic, the logic that disrupts this harmony through the mere fact of achieving the contingency of the equality, neither arithmetical nor geometric, of any speaking beings whatsoever.

In the initial conflict that produces a dispute about the deduction of the community of the just and the unjust from the capacity of any speaking being whatsoever, two logics of human being-together must therefore be discerned. These are generally confused with politics whereas political activity is none other than the activity that parcels them out. Politics is generally seen as the set of procedures whereby the aggregation and consent of collectivities is achieved, the organization of powers, the distribution of places and roles, and the systems for legitimizing this distribution. I propose to give this system of distribution and legitimization another name. I propose to call it *the police.*

This term no doubt poses a few problems. The word *police* normally evokes what is known as the petty police, the truncheon blows of the forces of law and order and the inquisitions of the secret police. But this narrow definition may be deemed contingent. Michel Foucault has shown that, as a mode of government, the police described by writers of the seventeenth and eighteenth centuries covered everything relating to "man" and his "happiness."[3] The petty police is just a particular form of a more general order that arranges that tangible reality in which bodies are distributed in community. It is the weakness and not the strength of this order in certain states that inflates the petty police to the point of putting it in charge of the whole set of police functions. The evolution of Western societies reveals *a contrario* that the policeman is one element in a social mechanism linking medicine, welfare, and culture. The policeman is destined to play the role of consultant and organizer as much as agent of public law and order, and no doubt the name itself will one day change, caught up as it will be in the process of euphemization through which our societies try to promote the image, at least, of all traditionally despised functions.

So from now on I will use the word *police* or *policing* as noun and adjective in this broader sense that is also "neutral," nonpejorative. I do not, however, identify the police with what is termed the "state apparatus." The notion of a state apparatus is in fact bound up with the presupposition of an opposition between State and society in which the state is portrayed as a machine, a "cold monster" imposing its rigid order on the life of society. This representation already presupposes a certain "political philosophy," that is, a certain confusion of politics and the police. The distribution of places and roles that defines a police regime stems as much from the assumed spontaneity of social relations as from the rigidity of state functions. The police is, essentially, the law, generally implicit, that defines a party's share or lack of it. But to define this, you first must define the configuration of the perceptible in which one or the other is inscribed. The police is thus first an order of bodies that defines the allocation of ways of doing, ways of being, and ways of saying, and sees that those bodies are assigned by name to a particular place and task; it is an order of the visible and the sayable that sees that a particular activity is visible and another is not, that this speech is understood as discourse and another as noise. It is police law, for example, that traditionally turns the workplace into a private space not regulated by the ways of seeing and saying proper to what is called the public domain, where the worker's *having a part* is strictly defined by the remuneration of his work. Policing is not so much the "disciplining" of bodies as a rule governing their appearing, a configuration of *occupations* and the properties of the spaces where these occupations are distributed.

I now propose to reserve the term *politics* for an extremely determined activity antagonistic to policing: whatever breaks with the tangible configuration whereby parties and parts or lack of them are defined by a presupposition that, by definition, has no place in that configuration—that of the part of those who have no part. This break is manifest in a series of actions that reconfigure the space where parties, parts, or lack of parts have been defined. Political activity is whatever shifts a body from the place assigned to it or changes a place's destination. It makes visible what had no business being seen, and makes heard a discourse where once there was only place for noise; it makes understood as discourse what was once only heard as noise. It might be the activity of Ballanche's plebeians who make use of a faculty for speech they do not "possess." It might be the activity of those nineteenth-century workers who established a collective basis for work relations that were solely the product of an infinite number of relationships between private individuals. Or again, the activity of demonstrators and those manning the barricades that literally turned urban communications paths into "public space." Spectacular or otherwise, political activity is always a mode of expression that undoes the perceptible divisions of the police order by implementing a basically heterogenous assumption, that of a part of those who have no part, an assumption that, at the end of the day, itself demonstrates the sheer contingency of the order, the equality of any speaking being with any other speaking being. Politics occurs when there is a place and a way for two heterogenous processes to meet. The first is the police process in the sense we have tried to define. The second is the process of equality. For the moment let's agree that this term means the open set of practices driven by the assumption of equality between any and every speaking being and by the concern to test this equality.

The formulation of this opposition obliges us to make a few further points and entails certain corollaries. First and foremost, the police order thus defined cannot be turned into that dim leveler in which everything looks the same, everything is equivalent ("at night all cows are grey"). The Scythians' practice of gouging out their slaves' eyes and the practices of modern information and communications strategies, which, conversely, put everything endlessly up for grabs, are both forms of police procedure. Which is not to say that we can draw from this the nihilistic conclusion that the one example is the same as the other. Our situation is in every way preferable to that of the Scythian slaves. There is a worse and a better police — the better one, incidentally, not being the one that adheres to the supposedly natural order of society or the science of legislators, but the one that all the breaking and entering perpetrated by egalitarian logic has most often jolted out of its "natural" logic. The police can procure all sorts of good, and one kind of police may be infinitely preferable to another. This does not change the nature of the police, which is what we are exclusively dealing with here. The regime of public opinion as gauged by the poll and of the unending exhibition of the real is today the normal form the police in Western societies takes. Whether the police is sweet and kind does not make it any less the opposite of politics.

It might be useful to set down what belongs to each sphere. For instance, lots of questions traditionally enlisted as concerning the relationship between morality and politics are really only concerned with the relationship between morality and the police. To decide whether any means are acceptable to ensure the tranquillity of the population and the security of the state is an issue that does not arise from political thought — which is not to say it can't provide the space for politics to sneak in sideways. Also, most of the measures that our clubs and political "think tanks" relentlessly come up with in a bid to change or revitalize politics by bringing the citizen closer to the state or the state closer to the citizen indeed offer the simplest alternative to politics: the simple police. For it is a representation of the community proper to the police that identifies citizenship as a property of individuals definable within a relationship of greater or lesser proximity between the place they occupy and that of public power. Politics, on the other hand, does not recognize relationships between citizens and the state. It only recognizes the mechanisms and singular manifestations by which a certain citizenship occurs but never belongs to individuals as such.

We should not forget either that if politics implements a logic entirely heterogenous to that of the police, it is always bound up with the latter. The reason for this is simple: politics has no objects or issues of its own. Its sole principle, equality, is not peculiar to it and is in no way in itself political. All equality does is lend politics reality in the form of specific cases to inscribe, in the form of litigation, confirmation of the equality at the heart of the police order. What makes an action political is not its object or the place where it is carried out, but solely its form, the form in which confirmation of equality is inscribed in the setting up of a dispute, of a community existing solely through being divided. Politics runs up against the police everywhere. We need to think of this encounter as a meeting of the heterogenous. To be able to do this we have to let go of certain concepts that assert in advance a smooth connection between them. The concept of power is the main such concept. This concept once allowed a certain well-meaning militancy to contend that "everything is political" since power relationships are everywhere. From that moment the somber vision of a power present everywhere and at every moment can be settled on, the heroic vision of politics as resistance or the dreamy vision of spaces of affirmative action opened up by those who turn their backs on politics and its power games. The concept of power allows one to retort with an "everything is policing" to an "everything is political," but this is pretty poor as a logical conclusion. If everything is political, then nothing is. So while it is important to show, as Michel Foucault has done magnificently, that the police order extends well beyond its specialized institutions and techniques, it is equally important to say that nothing is political in itself merely because power relationships are at work in it. For a thing to be political, it must give rise to a meeting of police logic and egalitarian logic that is never set up in advance.

So nothing is political in itself. But anything may become political if it gives rise to a meeting of these two logics. The same thing — an election, a strike, a demonstration — can give rise to politics or not give rise to politics. A strike is not political when it calls for reforms rather than a better deal or when it attacks the relationships of authority rather than the inadequacy of wages. It is political when it reconfigures the relationships that determine the workplace in its relation to the community. The domestic household has been turned into a political space not through the simple fact that power relationships are at work in it but because it was the subject of argument in a dispute over the capacity of women in the community. The same concept—opinion or law, for example—may define a structure of political action or a structure of the police order. Accordingly the same word "opinion" can define two opposing processes: the reproduction of governmental legitimizations in the form of the "feelings" of the governed or the setting up of a scene of conflict between this play of legitimizations and feelings; choosing from among responses proposed or the invention of a question that no one was asking themselves until then. But it should be added that such terms may also, and mostly do, designate the very entanglement of both logics. Politics acts on the police. It acts in the places and with the words that are common to both, even if it means reshaping those places and changing the status of those words. What is usually posited as the space of politics, meaning the set of state institutions, is precisely not a homogenous place. Its configuration is determined by the state of relations between political logic and police logic. But it is also, of course, the privileged space where their difference is dissimulated within the assumption of a direct link between the *arkhê* of the community and the distribution of the institutions, the *arkhaï* that effect its basis.

Nothing is political in itself for the political only happens by means of a principle that does not belong to it: equality. The status of this "principle" needs to be specified. Equality is not a given that politics then presses into service, an essence embodied in the law or a goal politics sets itself the task of attaining. It is a mere assumption that needs to be discerned within the practices implementing it. In the Aventine apologia, this assumption of equality is to be discerned even within a discourse proclaiming the fatal fact of inequality. Menenius Agrippa explains to the plebs that they are only the stupid members of a city whose soul is its patricians. But to teach the plebs their place this way he must assume they understand what he is saying. He must presume the equality of speaking beings, which contradicts the police distribution of bodies who are put in their place and assigned their role.

Let's grant one thing at the outset to those jaded spirits for whom equality rhymes with utopia while inequality evokes the healthy robustness of "the way it is": such an assumption is just as hollow as they reckon it is. In itself it has no particular effect, no political consistency. It may even be doubtful whether it could ever have such an effect or consistency. Moreover, those who have taken such doubt to its extreme are the greatest champions of equality. For politics to occur, there must be a meeting point between police logic and egalitarian logic. The consistency of this empty equality can itself only be an empty property, as is the freedom of the Athenians. The possibility or impossibility of politics is played out here, and this is where jaded spirits lose their bearings: for them, the empty notions of equality and liberty prevent politics. Now, the problem is strictly the reverse: for there to be politics, the apolitical structural vacuum of equality between anyone and everyone must produce the structural vacuum of a political property like the freedom of the demos of Athens.

This is a supposition that can be rejected. I have elsewhere analyzed the pure form of such a rejection in Joseph Jacotot, the theorist of the equality of intelligence and of intellectual emancipation.[4] Jacotot radically opposes the logic of the egalitarian assumption to the logic of the aggregation of social bodies. For Jacotot, it is always possible to make a show of this equality without which no inequality is thinkable, but on the strict condition that such an act is always a one-off performance, that it is every time the reproduction of the pure trace of its confirmation. This always one-off act of equality cannot consist in any form of social bond whatsoever. Equality turns into the opposite the moment it aspires to a place in the social or state organization. Intellectual emancipation accordingly cannot be institutionalized without becoming instruction of the people, in other words, a way of organizing the eternal minority. The two processes must remain absolutely alien to each other, constituting two radically different communities even if composed of the same individuals, the community of equal minds and that of social bodies lumped together by the fiction of inequality. They can never form a nexus except by transforming equality into the opposite. The equality of intelligence, the absolute condition of all communication and any social order, cannot have an impact in such an order by means of the empty freedom of some collective subject. Every individual in a society can be emancipated. But this emancipation — which is the modern term for the effect of equality — will never produce the vacuum of a freedom belonging to any demos or to any other subject of the kind. In the social order, there can be no vacuum. There is only ever the full, weights and counterweights. Politics is thus the name of nothing. It cannot be anything other than policing, that is, the denial of equality. The paradox of intellectual emancipation allows us to think the essential nexus of logos and wrong, the constitutive function of wrong in transforming egalitarian logic into political logic. Either equality has no effect on the social order or it has an effect in the specific form of wrong. The empty "freedom" that makes the poor of Athens the political subject, demos, is nothing more than the meeting of these two logics. It is nothing more than the wrong that institutes the community as a community based on conflict. Politics is the practice whereby the logic of the characteristic of equality takes the form of the processing of a wrong, in which politics becomes the argument of a basic wrong that ties in with some established dispute in the distribution of jobs, roles, and places. Politics occurs through specific subjects or mechanisms of subjectification. These measure the incommensurables, the logic of the mark of equality or that of the police order. They do this by uniting in the name of whatever social group the pure empty quality of equality between anyone and everyone, and by superimposing over the police order that structures the community another community that only exists through and for the conflict, a community based on the conflict over the very existence of something in common between those who have a part and those who have none.

Politics is a matter of subjects or, rather, modes of subjectification. By *subjectification* I mean the production through a series of actions of a body and a capacity for enunciation not previously identifiable within a given field of experience, whose identification is thus part of the reconfiguration of the field of experience. Descartes's *ego sum, ego existo* is the prototype of such indissoluble subjects of a series of operations implying the production of a new field of experience. Any political subjectification holds to this formula. It is a *nos sumus, nos existimus,* which means the subject it causes to exist has neither more nor less than the consistency of such a set of operations and such a field of experience. Political subjectification produces a multiple that was not given in the police constitution of the community, a multiple whose count poses itself as contradictory in terms of police logic. The commons, the people, are the first of these multiples that split up the community, the first inscription of a subject and a sphere where that subject appears as a backdrop for other modes of subjectification to inscribe other "existing bodies," other subjects of political conflict. A mode of subjectification does not create subjects ex nihilo; it creates them by transforming identities defined in the natural order of the allocation of functions and places into instances of experience of a dispute. "Workers" or "women" are identities that apparently hold no mystery. Anyone can tell *who* is meant. But political subjectification forces them out of such obviousness by questioning the relationship between a *who* and a *what* in the apparent redundancy of the positing of an existence. In politics "woman" is the subject of experience — the denatured, defeminized subject — that measures the gap between an acknowledged part (that of sexual complementarity) and a having no part. "Worker" or better still "proletarian" is similarly the subject that measures the gap between the part of work as social function and the having no part of those who carry it out within the definition of the common of the community. All political subjectification is the manifestation of a gap of this kind. The familiar police logic that decides that militant proletarians *are not* workers but déclassés, and that militant feminists are strangers to their sex, is, all in all, justified. Any subjectification is a disidentification, removal from the naturalness of a place, the opening up of a subject space where anyone can be counted since it is the space where those of no account are counted, where a connection is made between having a part and having no part. "Proletarian" political subjectification, as I have tried to show elsewhere, is in no way a form of "culture," of some collective ethos capable of finding a voice. It presupposes, on the contrary, a multiplicity of fractures separating worker bodies from their ethos and from the voice that is supposed to express the soul of this ethos: a multiplicity of speech events — that is, of one-off experiences of conflict over speech and voice, over the partition of the perceptible. "Speaking out" is not awareness and expression of a self asserting what belongs to it. It is the occupation of space in which the logos defines a nature other than the *phônê*. This occupation presupposes that the fates of "workers" are somehow turned around by an experience of the power of *logoï* in which resurrection of ancient political inscriptions can combine with the revealed secret of the Alexandrine. The modern political animal is first a literary animal, caught in the circuit of a literariness that undoes the relationships between the order of words and the order of bodies that determine the place of each. A political subjectification is the product of these multiple fracture lines by which individuals and networks of individuals subjectify the gap between their condition as animals endowed with a voice and the violent encounter with the equality of the logos.[5]

The difference that political disorder inscribes in the police order can thus, at first glance, be expressed as the difference between subjectification and identification. It inscribes a subject name as being different from any identified part of the community. This point may be illustrated by a historic episode, a speech scene that is one of the first political occurrences of the modern proletarian subject. It concerns an exemplary dialogue occasioned by the trial of the revolutionary Auguste Blanqui in 1832. Asked by the magistrate to give his profession, Blanqui simply replies: "proletarian." The magistrate immediately objects to this response: "That is not a profession," thereby setting himself up for copping the accused's immediate response: "It is the profession of thirty million Frenchmen who live off their labor and who are deprived of political rights."[6] The judge then agrees to have the court clerk list proletarian as a new "profession." Blanqui's two replies summarize the entire conflict between politics and the police: everything turns on the double acceptance of a single word, *profession*. For the prosecutor, embodying police logic, profession means job, trade: the activity that puts a body in its place and function. It is clear that proletarian does not designate any occupation whatever, at most the vaguely defined state of the poverty-stricken manual laborer, which, in any case, is not appropriate to the accused. But, within revolutionary politics, Blanqui gives the same word a different meaning: a profession is a profession of faith, a declaration of membership of a collective. Only, this collective is of a particular kind. The proletarian class in which Blanqui professes to line himself up is in no way identifiable with a social group. The proletariat are neither manual workers nor the labor classes. They are the class of the uncounted that only exists in the very declaration in which they are counted as those of no account. The name *proletarian* defines neither a set of properties (manual labor, industrial labor, destitution, etc.) that would be shared equally by a multitude of individuals nor a collective body, embodying a principle, of which those individuals would be members. It is part of a process of subjectification identical to the process of expounding a wrong. "Proletarian" subjectification defines a subject of wrong — by superimposition in relation to the multitude of workers. What is subjectified is neither work nor destitution, but the simple counting of the uncounted, the difference between an inegalitarian distribution of social bodies and the equality of speaking beings.

This is also why the wrong exposed by the name *proletarian* is in no way identical to the historically dated figure of the "universal victim" and its specific pathos. The wrong exposed by the suffering proletariat of the 1830s has the same logical structure as the *blaberon* implied in the unprincipled freedom of the Athenian demos, which had the audacity to identify itself with the whole of the community. It is just that in the case of Athenian democracy, this logical structure functions in its elementary form in the immediate unity of the demos as both part and whole. The proletarian declaration of membership, on the other hand, makes the gap between two peoples explicit: between the declared political community and the community that defines itself as being excluded from this community. "Demos" is the subject of the identity of the part and the whole. "Proletarian" on the contrary subjectifies the part of those who have no part that makes the whole different from itself. Plato railed against that demos that is the count of the uncountable. Blanqui, in the name of proletarians, inscribes the uncounted in a space where they are countable as uncounted. Politics in general is made up of such *miscounts;* it is the work of classes that are not classes that, in the particular name of a specific part or of the whole of the community (the poor, the proletariat, the people), inscribe the wrong that separates and reunites two heterogenous logics of the community. The concept of wrong is thus not linked to any theater of "victimization." It belongs to the original structure of all politics. Wrong is simply the mode of subjectification in which the assertion of equality takes its political shape. Politics occurs by reason of a single universal that takes the specific shape of wrong. Wrong institutes a singular universal, a polemical universal, by tying the presentation of equality, as the part of those who have no part, to the conflict between parts of society.

The founding wrong of politics is thus of a specific kind, and we should distinguish it from the figures with which it is usually assimilated, causing it to disappear in law, religion, or war. It is distinct first from the lawsuit, objectifiable as the relationship between specific parties that can be adjusted through appropriate legal procedures. Quite simply, parties do not exist prior to the declaration of wrong. Before the wrong that its name exposes, the proletariat has no existence as a real part of society. What is more, the wrong it exposes cannot be regulated by way of some accord between the parties. It cannot be regulated since the subjects a political wrong sets in motion are not entities to whom such and such has happened by accident, but subjects whose very existence is the mode of manifestation of the wrong. The persistence of the wrong is infinite because verification of equality is infinite and the resistance of any police order to such verification is a matter of principle. But though the wrong cannot be regulated, this does not mean that it cannot be processed. It is not the same as inexpiable war or irredeemable debt. Political wrong cannot be settled—through the objectivity of the lawsuit as a compromise between the parties. But it can be processed—through the mechanisms of subjectification that give it substance as an alterable relationship between the parties, indeed as a shift in the playing field.

The incommensurables of the equality of speaking beings and the distribution of social bodies are gauged in relation to each other, and

this gauge has an effect on the distribution itself. Between legal settle-
ment and inexpiable debt, the political dispute reveals an incompatibil-
ity that can nonetheless be processed. To simplify, this processing goes
beyond any dialogue concerning respective interests as well as any reciprocity of rights and duties. It passes through the constitution of specific subjects that take the wrong upon themselves, give it shape, invent
new forms and names for it, and conduct its processing in a specific
montage of *proofs:* "logical" arguments that are at the same time a way
of reshaping the relationship between speech and its *account* as well as
the perceptible configuration that demarcates the domains and powers
of the logos and the *phônê,* the spaces of the visible and the invisible,
and articulates these to the allocation of parties and parts. Political subjectification redefines the field of experience that gave to each their
identity with their lot. It decomposes and recomposes the relationships between the ways of *doing,* of *being,* and of *saying* that define the
perceptible organization of the community, the relationships between
the places where one does one thing and those where one does something else, the capacities associated with this particular *doing* and those
required for another. It asks if labor or maternity, for example, is a private or a social matter, if this social function is a public function or
not, if this public function implies a political capacity. A political subject
is not a group that "becomes aware" of itself, finds its voice, imposes
its weight on society. It is an operator that connects and disconnects
different areas, regions, identities, functions, and capacities existing in
the configuration of a given experience — that is, in the nexus of distri-
butions of the police order and whatever equality is already inscribed
there, however fragile and fleeting such inscriptions may be. A workers'
strike, for example, in its classic form, may bring together two things
that have "nothing to do" with one another: the equality proclaimed
by the Declaration of the Rights of Man and some obscure question
concerning hours of work or workshop regulation. The political act of
going out on strike then consists in building a relationship between
these things that have none, in causing the relationship and the nonrelationship to be seen together as the object of dispute. This construc-

tion implies a whole series of shifts in the order that defines the "part" of work: it presupposes that a number of relationships between one individual (the employer) and another individual (each of the employees) be posited as a collective relationship, that the private place of work be posited as belonging to the domain of public visibility, that the very status of the relationship between noise (machines, shouting, or suffering) and argumentative speech, configuring the place and part of work as a private relationship, be reconfigured. Political subjectification is an ability to produce these polemical scenes, these paradoxical scenes, that bring out the contradiction between two logics, by positing existences that are at the same time nonexistences — or nonexistences that are at the same time existences. Jeanne Deroin does this in exemplary fashion when, in 1849, she presents herself as a candidate for a legislative election in which she cannot run. In other words, she demonstrates the contradiction within a universal suffrage that excludes her sex from any such universality. She reveals herself and she reveals the subject "women" as necessarily included in the sovereign French people enjoying universal suffrage and the equality of all before the law yet being at the same time radically excluded. This demonstration is not a simple denunciation of an inconsistency or a lie regarding the universal. It is also the staging of the very contradiction between police logic and political logic which is at the heart of the republican definition of community. Jeanne Deroin's demonstration is not political in the sense in which she would say the home and housework are "political." The home and housework are no more political in themselves than the street, the factory, or government. Deroin's demonstration is political because it makes obvious the extraordinary imbroglio marking the republican relationship between the part of women and the very definition of the common of the community. The republic is both a regime founded on a declaration of equality that does not recognize any difference between the sexes and the idea of a complementarity in laws *and* morals. According to this complementarity, the part of women is that of morals and that education through which the minds and hearts of citizens are formed. Woman is mother and educator, not only of those future citizens who are her children but also, more important for the poor woman, of her husband. Domestic space is thus at once that private space, separated from the space of citizenship, and a space included in the complementarity of laws and morals that defines the accomplishment of citizenship. The unseemly appearance of a woman on the electoral stage transforms into a mode of exposure of a wrong, in the logical sense, this republican topos of laws and morals that binds police logic up in the definition of politics. By constructing the singular, polemical universality of a demonstration, it brings out the universal of the republic as a particularized universal, distorted in its very definition by the police logic of roles and parts. This means, conversely, that it transforms into arguments for the feminine *nos sumus, nos existimus* all these functions, "privileges," and capacities that police logic, thus politicized, attributes to women who are mothers, educators, carers, and civilizers of the class of lawmaker citizens.

In this way the bringing into relationship of two unconnected things becomes the measure of what is incommensurable between two orders: between the order of the inegalitarian distribution of social bodies in a partition of the perceptible and the order of the equal capacity of speaking beings in general. It is indeed a question of incommensurables. But these incommensurables are well gauged in regard to each other, and this gauge reconfigures the relationships of parts and parties, of objects likely to give rise to dispute, of subjects able to articulate it. It produces both new inscriptions of equality within liberty and a fresh sphere of visibility for further demonstrations. Politics is not made up of power relationships; it is made up of relationships between worlds.

Chapter 3

The Rationality of Disagreement

The incommensurable on which politics is based is not identifiable with any "irrationality." It is, rather, the very measure of the relationship between a logos and the *alogia* it defines — *alogia* in the double sense of the Greek of Plato and of Aristotle, signifying not only the animality of the creature simply doomed to the noise of pleasure and pain, but also the incommensurability that distinguishes the geometric order of good from the simple arithmetic of exchanges and allocations. Politics does indeed have a logic, but this logic is inevitably based on the very duality of the logos as speech and account of speech, and pinned down to the specific role of that logic: to make manifest *(deloun)* an *aisthêsis* that, as Ballanche's apologia has shown, was the space of distribution, of community, and of division. To lose sight of the double specificity of political "dialogue" is to lock oneself into false alternatives requiring a choice between the enlightenment of rational communication and the murkiness of inherent violence or irreducible difference. Political rationality is only thinkable precisely on condition that it be freed from the alternative in which a certain rationalism would like to keep it reined in, either as exchange between partners putting their interests or standards up for discussion, or else the violence of the irrational.

To posit such an alternative is to be a bit too quick to take as read what is in fact in question: identification of the discussion proper to political rationality and to its *manifestation* of what is just and unjust with a certain speech-act situation. The rationality of dialogue is thereby identified with the relationship between speakers addressing each other in the grammatical mode of the first and second persons in order to oppose each other's interests and value systems and to put the validity of these to the test. It is a bit too readily assumed that this constitutes an exact description of the forms of rational political logos and that it is thus, as a result, that justice forces its way into social relationships: through the meeting of partners who hear an utterance, immediately understand the act that caused it to be uttered, and take on board the intersubjective relationship that supports this understanding. Accordingly, linguistic pragmatics in general (the conditions required for an utterance to make sense and have an effect for the person uttering it) would provide the telos of reasonable and just exchange.

But is this really how the logos circulates within social relationships and makes an impact on them — through the identity between understanding and mutual understanding? One could, of course, say that this identification is a form of anticipation, a way of anticipating an ideal speaking situation, not yet given. Granted, a successful illocution is always anticipation of a speech situation that is not yet given; but it in no way follows from this that the vector of this anticipation is the identity between understanding and understanding. This vector is, on the contrary, the gap between two accepted meanings of "to understand" that institutes the rationality of political interlocution and establishes the type of "success" appropriate to it — which is not agreement between partners on the optimal allocation of parts, but the optimal way this partition is staged. Current usage suffices to teach us a curious fact of language: expressions containing the verb "to understand" are among those that most commonly need to be interpreted nonliterally and even, more often than not, to be understood strictly paradoxically. In ordinary social usage, an expression like "Do you understand?" is a false interrogative whose positive content is as follows: "There is nothing for you to understand, you don't need to understand" and even, possibly, "It's not up to you to understand; all you have to do is obey." "Do you understand?" is an expression that tells us precisely that "to understand" means two different, if not contrary, things: to understand a problem and to understand an order. In the logic of pragmatism, the speaker is obliged, for the success of their own performance, to submit it to conditions of validity that come from mutual understanding. Otherwise, the speaker falls into the "performative contradiction" that undermines the force of their utterance. "Do you understand?" is a performative that makes fun of the "performative contradiction" because its own performance, its manner of making itself understood, is to draw the line between two senses of the same word and two categories of speaking beings. This performative gives those it addresses to understand that there are people who understand problems and people who have only to understand the orders such people give them. It is a pointer to the partition of the perceptible, bringing off, without having to conceptualize it, the Aristotelian distinction between those who have only an *aisthêsis* of the logos and those who have its *hexis*.[1]

This is not to invoke the inexorability of a law of power that somehow always sets its seal in advance on the language of communication and stamps its violence on all rational argument. It is merely to note that the political rationality of argument can never be some simple clarification of what speaking means. To submit utterances to the conditions of their validity is to place in dispute the mode by which each party participates in the logos. A situation of political argument must always be won on the preexisting and constantly reenacted distribution of the language of problems and the language of commands. "Do you understand?" is not the dark night of power in which the capacity to argue will run aground—particularly the capacity to argue about right. But it forces us to see the scene as more complicated, and the response to "Do you understand?" will necessarily become more complex. The person thus addressed will respond at several levels on pondering the utterance and its double meaning. At an initial level, they will respond: "We understand because we understand," which means: "Since we understand your orders, we share with you the same faculty of understanding." At the next level, though, this tautology gets complicated precisely by bringing out — sharing as a dispute — the gap presupposed by the question: the gap between the language of command and the language of problems, which is also the gap within the logos, one distinguishing understanding of an utterance and understanding the count of each person's words this understanding implies. The response will therefore become complicated accordingly: "We understand what you say when you say 'Do you understand?' We understand that in saying 'Do you understand?' you are in fact saying: 'There's no need for you to understand me, you don't have the wherewithal to understand me, and so on.'"

But this second-degree understanding may itself be understood and universalized in two opposing ways, depending on how it articulates the community and noncommunity implied by the gap between the capacity to speak and the account of the words spoken. The first possibility makes this account the ultimate way of interpreting the meaning of the utterance. We might sum it up like this: "We understand that you are using the medium of communication to impose your language on us. We understand that you are lying when you posit the language of your commands as a common language. We understand, in short, that all universals in language and communication are merely a lure, that there are only idioms of power, and that we, too, must forge our own." The second possibility would argue the reverse, making community (of capacity) the ultimate reason for noncommunity (of the account): "We understand that you wish to signify to us that there are two languages and that we cannot understand you. We perceive that you are doing this in order to divide the world into those who command and those who obey. We say on the contrary that there is a single language common to us and that consequently we understand you even if you don't want us to. In a word, we understand that you are lying by denying there is a common language."

The response to the false question "Do you understand?" thus implies the constitution of a specific speech scene in which it is a matter of constructing another relationship by making the position of the enunciator

THE RATIONALITY OF DISAGREEMENT

explicit. The utterance thereby completed then finds itself extracted from the speech situation in which it functioned naturally. It is placed in another situation in which it no longer works, in which it is the object of scrutiny, reduced to the status of an utterance in a common language. Within this space of the commentary that objectifies and universalizes the "functional" utterance, the utterance's claims to validity are thoroughly put to the test. In setting up the common dispute proper to politics, the *cum* of the *commentary* that objectifies the gap between the logos and itself, within the polemical gap of a first and third person, is indistinguishable from the gap in *communication* between a first and a second person. No doubt it is a distrust of this shift between persons that frustrates Jürgen Habermas's efforts to distinguish the rational argument that creates community from simple discussion and the putting together of particular interests. In *The Philosophical Discourses of Modernity,* Habermas accuses his opponents of adopting the point of view of the observer, of the third person, on the argument and communication front; this freezes rational communication, which does its work in the play of a first person engaged in embracing the second-person point of view.[2] But such an opposition locks the rational argument of political debate into the same speech situation as the one it seeks to overcome: the simple rationality of a dialogue of interests. In underestimating this multiplication of persons associated with the multiplication of the political logos, Habermas also forgets that the third person is as much a person of direct and indirect speech as a person of observation and objectification. He forgets that one commonly speaks to partners in the third person, not only in several languages' formulas of politeness, but whenever the relationship between speakers is posited as the very stakes of the interlocutionary situation. Our theater summarizes this gambit in a few exemplary exchanges, such as the dialogue in Molière's *The Miser* between the cook/coachman of Harpagon, the miser, and his steward:

> "Master Jacques is a great talker.
> —And Master Steward is a great meddler!"

Such theatrical conflicts, which are domestic conflicts, aptly demonstrate the connection between the "third person of politeness" and that third person of identification that institutionalizes social conflict, the third person of the workers' representative who declares, "Workers will not accept..." It would be missing the logic of the play of persons implied here if one were to reduce this third person enunciated by a first person either to the natural ("animal") process of the *aisthêsis* of a collective body that finds its voice, or to some kind of deceptive identification with an impossible or missing collective body. The play of the third person is essential to the logic of political discussion, which is never a simple dialogue. It is always both less and more: less, for it is always in the form of a monologue that the dispute, the gap internal to the logos, declares itself, and more, for commentary sets off a multiplication of persons. In such an interchange, the "they" plays a triple role. First, it designates the other person as the one with whom not only a conflict of interests is under debate but the very situation of the speakers as speaking beings. Second, it addresses a third person at whose door it virtually lays this question. Third, it sets up the first person, the "I" or "we" of the speaker, as representative of a community. In politics, it is the set of these interactions that is meant by "public opinion." *Political* public opinion (as distinct from police management of state legitimization processes) is not primarily some network of enlightened minds discussing common problems. Rather, it is an informed opinion of a particular kind: an opinion that evaluates the very manner in which people speak to each other and how much the social order has to do with the fact of speaking and its interpretation. This explains the historical connection between the fate of certain valets in comedy and the development of the very notion of public opinion.

At the heart of all arguing and all litigious argument of a political nature lies a basic quarrel as to what understanding language implies. Clearly, all interlocution supposes comprehension of some kind of content of the illocution. The contentious issue is whether this understanding presupposes a telos of mutual understanding. By "contentious issue" I mean two things: first, that there is an assumption here that remains to be proven, but also that it is precisely here that the original dispute, at play in all specific litigious arguments, lies. Any interlocutionary situation is split at the outset by the contentious issue — unresolved and conflictual — of knowing what can be deduced from the understanding of a language.

We can deduce either something or nothing from such an understanding. From the fact that a command is understood by an inferior we can simply deduce that such a command was indeed given, that the person giving orders has succeeded in their work, and that as a result the person receiving the order will indeed carry out their own work, the extension of the former, in keeping with the division between simple *aisthêsis* and the fullness of *hexis*. Another, completely contrary, deduction can also be made: the inferior has understood the superior's order because the inferior takes part in the same community of speaking beings and so is, in this sense, their equal. In short, we can deduce that the inequality of social ranks works only because of the very equality of speaking beings.

This deduction is upsetting, in the proper sense of the term. Whenever it is opted for, it is clear societies have long been ticking over. And what makes them tick is the idea that the understanding of language has no bearing on the definition of the social order. With their functions and their commands, their allocations of parts and parties, societies work on the basis of an idea that the most basic logic seems to confirm — namely, that inequality exists because of inequality. The consequence is that the logic of understanding "normally" only presents itself in the form of a subversive paradox and endless conflict. To say that there is a common speech situation *because* an inferior understands what a superior is saying means that a disagreement, a provisional confrontation, must be set up between two camps: those who think there is an understanding within understanding, that is, that all speaking beings are equal as speaking beings, and those who do not think so. The paradox is that those who think there is an understanding within understanding are for that very reason unable to take this deduction any further except in the form of conflict, of disagreement, since they are bound to show a result that is not at all apparent. The political stage, the theater of a paradoxical community that places the dispute in common, therefore cannot possibly be identified with a model of communication between established partners concerning objects and ends belonging to a common language. This does not mean that the political stage is reduced to the incommunicability of languages, an impossibility of understanding linked to the heterogeneity of language games. Political interlocution has always mixed up language games and rules of expression, and it has always particularized the universal in demonstrative sequences comprised of the meeting of heterogeneous elements. Comprehensible narratives and arguments have always been composed of language games and heterogeneous rules of expression. The problem is not for people speaking "different languages," literally or figuratively, to understand each other, any more than it is for "linguistic breakdowns" to be overcome by the invention of new languages. The problem is knowing whether the subjects who count in the interlocution "are" or "are not," whether they are speaking or just making a noise. It is knowing whether there is a case for seeing the object they designate as the visible object of the conflict. It is knowing whether the common language in which they are exposing a wrong is indeed a common language. The quarrel has nothing to do with more or less transparent or opaque linguistic contents; it has to do with consideration of speaking beings as such. This is why there is no call for contrasting some modern age of litigation, associated with the great narrative of modern times and with the drama of the universal victim, to a modern age of differend, associated with the contemporary explosion of language games and small-scale narratives.[3] The heterogeneity of language games is not an inevitability for contemporary societies that suddenly comes and puts an end to the great narrative of politics. On the contrary, it is constitutive of politics, it is what distinguishes politics from equal juridical and commercial exchange on the one hand and, on the other, from the alterity of religion and war.

This is the significance of the scene on the Aventine. This exceptional scene is not just a "tale of origins." Such "origins" never stop repeating themselves. Ballanche's narrative is presented in the unusual form of a retrospective prophecy: a moment in Roman history is reinterpreted in a way that transforms it into a prophecy of the historic destiny of peoples in general. But this retrospective prophecy is also an anticipation of the immediate future. Ballanche's text appeared in the *Revue de Paris* between the spring and fall of 1829. In the meantime, the July Revolution had broken out in Paris, looking to many like the demonstration *hic et nunc* of that "general rule for all peoples" of which Ballanche spoke. And that revolution was followed by a whole series of social movements that took on exactly the same form as that of Ballanche's tale. The names of the actors, sets, and props might change, but the rule remains the same. It consists of creating a stage around any specific conflict on which the equality or inequality as speaking beings of the partners in the conflict can be played out. Doubtless, at the time Ballanche was writing his apologue, it had ceased to be said that the members of the modern proletariat, the equivalent of the plebeians of antiquity, *are not* speaking beings. It is simply assumed that there is no connection between the fact that they speak and the fact that they work. There is no need to explain why there is no connection; it suffices not to see the connection. Those who make the existing order work, either as rulers, magistrates, or governors, can't see the connection between one term and the other. They can't see the middle term between two identities that might be joined together in the speaking being, who shares a common language, and the laborer, who exercises a specific occupation as an employee in a factory or works for a manufacturer. As a result, they don't see how the lot a laborer receives by way of a wage might become the business of the community, the object of public discussion.

And so the quarrel always bears on the prejudicial question: is there any call for the common world of speaking on this subject to be set up? The disagreement that becomes entrenched in the years following Ballanche's apologue, this disagreement that will be called a social movement or the workers' movement, consisted in saying that this common world existed; that the status common to the speaking being in general and to the laborer employed in whatever specific function existed; and that this common status was also common to the workers and their employers, that it consisted of their belonging to the same sphere of community, already recognized, already written down — even if in idealistic and fleeting inscriptions: that of the revolutionary declaration of the equality in law of man and the citizen. The disagreement destined to put this understanding into action consisted in asserting that the inscription of equality in the form of "the equality of man and the citizen" before the law defined a sphere of community and publicness that included the "business" of work and determined the place where work is performed as arising from public discussion among specific subjects.

This assertion implies a most peculiar platform of argument. The worker subject that gets included on it as speaker has to behave *as though* such a stage existed, as though there were a common world of argument — which is eminently reasonable *and* eminently unreasonable, eminently wise and resolutely subversive, since such a world does not exist. The workers' strikes of the time derive their peculiar discursive structure by exacerbating this paradox: they are keen to show that it is indeed as reasonable speaking beings that workers go on strike, that the act that causes them to all stop working together is not a *noise,* a violent reaction to a painful situation, but the expression of a logos, which not only is the inventory of a power struggle but constitutes a *demonstration* of their right, a *manifestation* of what is just that can be understood by the other party.

Workers' manifestos of the time accordingly reveal a remarkable discursive ordering, the main feature of which can be schematized as follows: "Here are our arguments. You can, or rather, 'they' can recognize them. Anyone can recognize them." This demonstration simultaneously addresses both the "they" of public opinion and the "they" given to it. Of course, such recognition does not occur because what the demonstration itself presupposes is not recognized, meaning that there is a common world in the form of a public space in which two groups of speaking beings, the bosses and the workers, might exchange their arguments. But the world of work is supposed to be a private realm where one individual proposes conditions to any number of individuals who each either accepts or rejects them. From that moment, no arguments can be received because they are addressed by subjects who do not exist to subjects who also do not exist in relation to a common equally nonexistent object. There is only a revolt there, the noise of aggravated bodies. All that is required is to wait for it to stop or to ask the authorities to make it stop.

The discursive ordering of the conflict is then developed by a second feature, a second movement: "We are right to argue for our rights and so to posit the existence of a common world of argument. And we are right to do so precisely because those who ought to recognize it do not, because they act as though they are ignorant of the existence of this common world." It is in this second movement of the argument's structure that the objectifying function of commentary plays an essential role. The workers' manifestos of the day comment on the speech of the bosses, used only to call for repression on the part of public powers, the speech of judges who condemn, or the speech of journalists who comment, in order to demonstrate that the words of such people go against the *evidence* of a common world of reason and argument. They thereby demonstrate that the speech of the masters or magistrates who deny the right of the workers to strike is a confirmation of this right *because* such words imply a noncommunity, an inequality that is impossible, contradictory. If the "performative contradiction" may intervene here, it is at the heart of this situation of argument that must first take no notice of it in order to clearly show its ignorance.

Let's suppose we have a situation of disagreement of this kind, transposing Ballanche's scene into a workers' dispute. At first, through use of the third person of public opinion, the argument situates the scene of disagreement, which means qualifying the relationship between the parties: the noise of revolt or speech that exposes a wrong.

"These gentlemen treat us with contempt. They urge the powers that be to persecute us; they dare accuse us of *revolt*. But are we therefore their niggers? Revolt! when we ask that our rates be raised, when we join together to abolish the exploitation of which we are the victims, to soften the hardships of our condition! Verily there is shamelessness in the word. It alone justifies the course we have resolved to take."[4]

The tone of the bosses' letter, which describes the strike-demonstration as a revolt, justifies the demonstration, since it shows that the masters are not talking about those they employ as speaking beings joined to them by understanding the same language, but as noisy animals or slaves capable only of understanding orders, since it also shows that the not being taken into account implied in their manner of speaking is a nonright. The platform of disagreement being thereby established, it is possible to argue *as though* this discussion between partners, which is challenged by the other party, had really taken place; in short, it is possible to establish, by reasoning and reckoning, the validity of the workers' revindications. And once this demonstration of the "right" of the strikers is complete, it is possible to add a second demonstration, one derived precisely from the refusal to take such a right into account, to embrace it in the name of speech that counts.

> "Do we need further proof of our right? Note the tone of the letter these gentlemen have written . . . In vain do they end by talking of moderation: we understand them all right."[5]

This "we understand them all right" nicely sums up what to understand means in a political structure of disagreement. Such comprehension implies a complex structure of interlocution that doubly reconstructs a scene of community doubly denied. But this scene of community only exists in the relationship of an "us" to a "them." And this relationship is just as much a nonrelationship. It doubly includes in the argument situation he who rejects its existence — and who is justified in the existing order of things in rejecting its existence. It includes him initially in the supposition that he is indeed included in the situation, that he is capable of understanding the argument (and that, anyway, he does understand it since he can't come up with a reply). It includes him in it as

54

the second person implicit in a dialogue. And it includes him a second time in the demonstration of the fact that he is trying to escape from the situation, trying not to understand the argument and perform the nominations and descriptions adequate to a situation of discussion between speaking beings.

In any social discussion in which there is actually something to discuss, this structure is implicated, a structure in which the place, the object, and the subjects of the discussion are themselves in dispute and must in the first instance be tested. Before any confrontation of interests and values, before any assertions are submitted to demands for validation between established partners, there is the dispute over the object of the dispute, the dispute over the existence of the dispute and the parties confronting each other in it. For the idea that speaking beings are equal because of their common capacity for speech is a reasonable-unreasonable idea — unreasonable, in regard to the way societies are structured, from the holy kingdoms of Antiquity to our modern societies of experts. The assertion of a common world thus happens through a paradoxical mise-en-scène that brings the community and the noncommunity together. And such a conjunction always arises from paradox and the scandal that overturns legitimate situations of communication, the legitimate parceling out of worlds and languages, and that redistributes the way speaking bodies are distributed in an articulation between the order of saying, the order of doing, and the order of being. The *demonstration* of right or *manifestation* of what is just is a reconfiguring of the partition of the perceptible. In the words of Jürgen Habermas, this demonstration is indissolubly a communicational intervention, bringing into play certain utterances' claims to validity and a strategic intervention, shifting the power struggle that determines whether utterances can be received as arguments on a common stage. Such communication also eludes the distinctions on which the supposedly "normal" rules of discussion are based. In *The Philosophical Discourses of Modernity,* Habermas insists on the tension between two kinds of linguistic acts: "poetic" languages that open the world up and the closed-world forms of arguing and validating. He accuses those he criticizes with underrating this tension and the necessity for aesthetic languages that open the world up and also legitimize themselves within the rules of communicating.[6]

But the point is that the *demonstration* proper to politics is always both argument and opening up the world where argument can be received and have an impact — argument about the very existence of such a world. And this is where the question of the universal comes in, before playing its part in issues such as whether universalization of interests is possible or impossible and how different forms of argument can be checked in a supposedly normal situation. The first requirement of universality is that speaking beings universally belong to the linguistic community; it is always dealt with in "abnormal" communication situations, in situations that introduce cases. Such polemical situations are those in which one of the partners of the interlocution refuses to recognize one of its features (its place, its object, its subjects). The universal is always at stake here in a peculiar way, in the form of cases whereby its very existence and pertinence are in dispute. It is always at stake locally and polemically, both as compelling and as not compelling. It must first be acknowledged and be made to be acknowledged that a situation presents a compelling case of universality. And this recognition allows no division between a rational order of argument from a poetic, if not irrational, order of commentary and metaphor. It is produced by linguistic acts that are at the same time rational arguments and "poetic" metaphors.

Indeed it needs to be said, paraphrasing Plato, "without shying away from it": the forms of social interlocution that have any impact are at once arguments in a situation and metaphors of this situation. That argument is in community with metaphor and metaphor with argument does not in itself entail any of the disastrous consequences sometimes described. This community is not one of the discoveries of exhausted modernity, which would then denounce the universality of social debate and conflict as an artifact produced by a major narrative. The argument linking two ideas and the metaphor revealing a thing in another thing have always been in community. It is just that this community is more or less binding according to different spheres of rationality and speech situations. There are spheres in which it may be reduced to practically nothing; these are areas where the assumption of understanding poses no problem, where it is assumed either that everyone understands each other or can understand each other as to what is being said, or that this just does not matter. The first case is that of symbolic languages that do not refer to anything outside themselves; the second is what happens with chatting, which can freely refer to anything at all. On the other hand, there are other areas in which such community peaks. These are those areas where the assumption of understanding is in dispute, where it is necessary to simultaneously produce both the argument and the situation in which it is to be understood, the object of the discussion and the world in which it features as object.

Political interlocution is one such area par excellence. Having to do with the very nexus of the logos and its *being taken into account* with the *aisthêsis* (the partition of the perceptible), its logic of *demonstration* is indissolubly an aesthetic of *expression*. Politics did not have the misfortune of being aestheticized or spectacularized just the other day. The aesthetic configuration in which what the speaking being says leaves its mark has always been the very stakes of the dispute that politics enlists in the police order. This says a lot for how wrong it is to identify "aesthetics" with the sphere of "self-referentiality" that sidetracks the logic of interlocution. "Aesthetics" is on the contrary what allows separate regimes of expression to be pooled. It is true, though, that the modern history of political brands is linked to those mutations that have emphasized aesthetics as partition of the perceptible as well as discourse on the perceptible. The modern emergence of aesthetics as an autonomous discourse determining an autonomous division of the perceptible is the emergence of an evaluation of the perceptible that is distinct from any judgment about the use to which it is put; and which accordingly defines a world of virtual community — of community demanded — superimposed on the world of commands and lots that gives everything a use. That a palace may be the object of an evaluation that has no bearing on the convenience of a residence, the privileges of a role, or the emblems of a majesty, is what, for Kant, particularizes the aesthetic community and the requirement of universality proper to it.[7] So the autonomization of aesthetics means first freeing up the norms of representation, and second, constituting a kind of community of sense experience that works on the world of assumption, of the *as if* that includes those who are not included by revealing a mode of existence of sense experience that has eluded the allocation of parties and lots.

There never has been any "aestheticization" of politics in the modern age because politics is aesthetic in principle. But the autonomization of aesthetics as a new nexus between the order of the logos and the partition of the perceptible is part of the modern configuration of politics. The politics of Antiquity was played out in vague notions such as *doxa,* as the *appearance* that sets the people up in the position of the community's *deciding* subject [*dokein:* to judge, decide]. Modern politics is first played out in this distinct notion of a virtual or due community of sense experience beyond the distribution of commands and jobs. Ancient politics held to the sole notion of the demos and its improper properties, opening up public space as the space of dispute. Modern politics holds to the multiplication of those operations of subjectification that invent worlds of community that are worlds of dissension; it holds to those demonstration devices that are, every time, at once arguments and world openers, the opening up of common (which does not mean consensual) worlds where the subject who argues is counted as an arguer. This subject is always a *one-over.* The subject writing in our manifesto "We understand them all right" is not the collection of workers, not a collective body. It is a surplus subject defined by the whole set of operations that *demonstrate* such an understanding by *manifesting* its distancing structure, its structure of relationship between the common and the not common. Modern politics exists through the multiplication of the common/litigious worlds deductible over the surface of social activities and orders. It exists through the subjects that this multiplication authorizes, subjects whose count is always supernumerary. The politics of Antiquity held to the sole miscount of that demos that is both part and whole, and of the freedom that belongs exclusively to it while belonging to everyone at the same time. Modern politics holds to the deployment of dispute subjectification devices that link the count of the uncounted to the distance from oneself of every subject capable of articulating it. It is not just that citizens, workers, or women designated in a sequence of the type "we citizens," "we workers," or "we women" cannot be identified with any collection, any social group. It is also that the relationship of the "we," the subject of the utterance that opens the sequence, to the subject announced, whose identity is served up in a variety of forms (citizens, workers, women, proletarians), is defined solely by the set of relationships and operations in the demonstrative sequence. Neither the *we* or the identity assigned to it, nor the apposition of the two defines a subject. There are political subjects or rather modes of subjectification only in the set of relationships that the *we* and its *name* maintain with the set of "persons," the complete play of identities and alterities implicated in the demonstration and the worlds — common or separate — where these are defined.

No doubt the demonstration operates more clearly when the names of subjects are distinct from any social group identifiable as such. When the dissidents of the Eastern Bloc adopted the term "hooligans" with which they were stigmatized by the heads of these regimes, when demonstrators in the Paris of 1968 declared, against all police evidence, "We are all German Jews," they exposed for all to see the gap between political subjectification — defined in the nexus of a logical utterance and an aesthetic manifestation — and any kind of identification. Politics' penchant for dialogue has much more to do with literary heterology, with its utterances stolen and tossed back at their authors and its play on the first and third persons, than with the allegedly ideal situation of dialogue between a first and a second person. Political invention operates in acts that are at once argumentative and poetic, shows of strength that open again and again, as often as necessary, worlds in which such acts of community are acts of community. This is why the "poetic" is not opposed here to argument. It is also why the creation of litigious, aesthetic worlds is not the mere invention of languages appropriate to reformulating problems that cannot be dealt with in existing languages.

59

In *Contingency, Irony, and Solidarity,* Richard Rorty distinguishes ordinary communication situations where there is agreement, more or less, on what is being discussed and exceptional situations where the themes and terms of the discussion are themselves open to debate.[8] Such situations would cover poetic moments in which creators form new languages enabling common experience to be described differently or invent new metaphors that are later called on to enter the arenas of common linguistic tools and of consensual reality. According to Rorty, then, we could elaborate an accord between the creation of poetic metaphor and liberal consensuality: a consensuality that is not exclusive since it is the sedimentation of old metaphors and old inventions of poetic irony. But exclusive consensus comes unstuck not only at exceptional moments and through specialists in irony. It comes unstuck as often as specific worlds of community open up, worlds of disagreement and dissension. Politics occurs wherever a community with the capacity to argue and to make metaphors is likely, at any time and through anyone's intervention, to crop up.

Chapter 4

From Archipolitics to Metapolitics

We can now determine the relationship between philosophy and politics implied in the term "political philosophy." The term "political philosophy" does not designate any genre, any territory or specification of philosophy. Nor does it designate politics' reflection on its immanent rationality. It is the name of an encounter — and a polemical encounter at that — in which the paradox or scandal of politics is exposed: its lack of any proper foundation. Politics only exists through the bringing off of the equality of anyone and everyone in a vacuous freedom of a part of the community that deregulates any count of parts. The equality that is the nonpolitical condition of politics does not show up here for what it is: it only appears as the figure of wrong. Politics is always distorted by the refraction of equality in freedom. It is never pure, never based on some essence proper to the community and the law. It only occurs when the community and the law change in status through the addition of equality to the law (the *isonomy* of Athens is not the simple fact that the law is "equal for everyone" but the fact that the purpose of the law is to represent equality) and through the emergence of a part identical to the whole.

"Political philosophy" begins with the revelation of this scandal, and this revelation is conducted by means of an idea presented as an alternative to the unfounded state of politics. It is the watchword Socrates uses to express his difference from the men of the democratic city: to really do politics, to do politics in truth, to engage in politics as a way of bringing off the exclusive essence of politics. The watchword supposes a certain observed fact and a certain diagnosis: the observed fact is that of politics' always prior factuality with regard to any principle of community. It is first in relation to politics that philosophy, from the very beginning, "comes too late." Only for philosophy this "lateness" is the wrong of democracy. In the form of democracy, politics is already in place, without waiting for its theoretical underpinnings or its *arkhê*, without waiting for the proper beginning that will give birth to it as performance of its own principle. The demos is already there with its three features: the erecting of a sphere for the name of the people to appear; the unequal count of this people that is both whole and part at the same time; the paradoxical revelation of the dispute by a part of the community that identifies with the whole in the very name of the wrong that makes it the other party. This observation of the fact of antecedence is transformed by "political philosophy" into a diagnosis of inherent vice. Democracy's antecedence becomes its sheer factuality or facticity, its regulation by rule alone (deregulation alone) of the empirical circulation of good and bad, pleasure and pain; by the sole equality (the sole inequality) of more and less. As far as justice goes, democracy only offers the theatrics of dispute. Offering a justice bogged down in the various forms of dispute and an equality flattened by the arithmetical counts of inequality, democracy is incapable of giving politics its true measure. Political philosophy's inaugural discourse can then be summed up in two phrases: first, equality is not democracy, and second, justice is not management of wrong.

In their own blunt way, these two propositions are correct. Equality does not in fact show up in democracy or justice in wrong. Politics is always at work on the gap that makes equality consist solely in the figure of wrong. It works at the meeting point of police logic and the logic of equality. But the whole problem is knowing how to interpret this gap. Now, with Plato, polemical philosophy turns it into the sign of a radical falseness. Plato declares that any politics that is not a performance of its own principle, not an embodiment of a principle of community, is no politics at all. "Politics in truth" then emerges and opposes the *krateïn* of the demos and substitutes for its specific torsion a pure logic of *either–or*, of the stark alternative between the divine model and the perishable model. The harmony of justice then opposes wrong, reduced to the chicanery of pettifogging lawyers with twisted minds; geometric equality, as the proportion of the cosmos appropriate to bringing the soul of the city into line, opposes a democratic equality reduced to arithmetical equality — that is, to the reign of the more or less. Faced with the unthinkable political nexus of the equal and the unequal, the program of political philosophy (or rather, of the politics of the philosophers) is defined as the achievement of the true essence of politics, of which democracy merely produces the appearance, and the elimination of this impropriety, this distance from itself of the community that the democratic political apparatus sets up in the very heart of the space of the city. The solution, in a word, is to achieve the essence of politics by eliminating this difference from itself that politics consists of, to achieve politics by eliminating politics, by achieving philosophy "in place" of politics.

But eliminating politics as an achievement, putting the true notion of community and the good attached to its nature in place of the distortion of equality as wrong, means first eliminating the difference between politics and the police. The basis of the politics of the philosophers is the identity of the principle of politics as an activity with that of the police as a way of determining the partition of the perceptible that defines the lot of individuals and parties. The inaugural conceptual act of such a politics is Plato's splitting a notion in two, the notion of *politeia*. The way Plato sees it, this is not a constitution, a general form that then splinters into permutations — democracy, oligarchy, or tyranny. It is the alternative to these alternations. On the one hand, there is the *politeia;* on the other, *politeiaï,* the sundry varieties of bad regimes bound up with the conflict between parts of the city and with the domination of one part over the others. The evil, says book VIII of the *Laws*, lies with these *politeiaï*, none of which is a *politeia*, all of which are mere factions, governments of discord.[1] The Platonic *politeia* is the regime of the community's interiority as opposed to the vicious circle of bad regimes. The *politeia* is opposed to the *politeiaï* as the One of the community is opposed to the multiple of combinations of wrong. Even Aristotelian "realism" acknowledges the *politeia* as the good state of the community of which democracy is a deviant form. This is because the *politeia* is the regime of community based on its essence, the one in which all manifestations of the common stem from the same principle. Those who today contrast the good republic with a dubious democracy are more or less consciously heirs to this initial separation. The *republic* or *politeia*, as Plato invents it, is a community functioning within the regime of the Same, expressing the principle and telos of community in all the activities of the different parts of society. The *politeia* is first a regime, a way of life, a mode of politics, that is like the life of an organism regulated by its own law, breathing at its own pace, charging each of its parts with the vital principle that destines it to its own role and good. The *politeia*, as Plato conceives it, is a community achieving its own principle of interiority in all manifestations of its life. It is wrong made impossible. To put it simply: the *politeia* of the philosophers is the exact identity of politics and the police.

This identity has two aspects. On the one hand, the politics of the philosophers identifies politics with the police. It places it in the regime of the One distributed as parts and roles. It incorporates the community in the assimilation of its laws to ways of life, to the principle of the breathing of a living body. But this incorporation does not mean that political philosophy comes down to the naturalness of policing. Political philosophy exists because this naturalness is lost, the age of Khronos is behind us, and, anyway, its much-trumpeted blissfulness celebrates only the imbecility of a vegetative existence. Political philosophy — or the politics of the philosophers — exists because the division is there, because democracy offers the paradox of a specific incommensurable, of the part of those who have no part, as a problem for philosophy to solve. *Isonomy* has already passed this way, already done its work here — meaning, the idea that the specific law of politics is a law based on an equality that opposes any natural law of domination. The *Republic* is not restoration of the virtue of bygone times; it is a solution to the logical problem with which democracy goads philosophy, the paradox of the part of those who have no part. To identify politics with the police may also mean identifying the police with politics, constructing an imitation of politics. To imitate the idea of good, the *politeia* then imitates the "bad" politics for which its imitation is supposed to be a substitute. Political philosophies, at least those worthy of the name, the name of this particular paradox, are philosophies that offer a solution to the paradox of the part of those who have no part, either by substituting an equivalent role for it, or by creating a simulacrum of it, by performing an imitation of politics in negating it. On the basis of this double aspect of identity the three great figures of political philosophy are defined, the three great figures of the conflict between philosophy and politics and of the paradox of the achievement-elimination of politics, whose last word may well be the achievement-elimination of philosophy itself. I call these three great figures *archipolitics, parapolitics*, and *metapolitics*.

Archipolitics, whose model is supplied by Plato, reveals in all its radicality the project of a community based on the complete realization of the *arkhê* of community, total awareness, replacing the democratic configuration of politics with nothing left over. To replace this configuration with nothing left over means offering a logical solution to the paradox of the part of those who have no part. This solution involves a rule that has to do not only with proportionality but with inverse proportionality. The founding narrative of the three races and the three metals in book III of the *Republic* not only establishes the hierarchical order of the city where the head rules the stomach; it also establishes a city where the superiority, the *kratos* of the best over the less good, does not signify any relationship of domination, no *cracy* in the political sense. For this to happen, the *kratein* of the best must be achieved as an inverse distribution of lots. So that magistrates, who have gold in their souls, cannot have any material gold in their hands, means their own share can only be the common lot. Their "entitlement" being knowledge of the friendship of celestial bodies that the community should imitate, their own lot can only be what is common to the community. Symmetrically, the common lot of artisans is to have as their share only what is their own: the houses and gold they alone have the right to own are the currency of their specific participation in the community. They participate in the community only on condition of not interfering in the affairs of the community in any way. They are only members of the community thanks to making the works for which nature has exclusively intended them (shoemaking, building frames for houses, or whatever other manual labor) — or rather, thanks to only performing their function, to having no other space-time than what is required by their trade.

Of course, what is suppressed by this law of exclusivity, presented as a proper and natural characteristic of the practice of any trade, is this common space that democracy carves out in the heart of the city as the place where liberty is to be exercised, the place where the power of the demos that brings off the part of those who have no part is to be exercised. And it is this paradoxical time that those who do not have the time devote to such a practice. The apparently empirical nature of the beginning of the *Republic*, with its counting of needs and functions, is an initial resolution of the paradox of democracy: the demos is broken down into its members so that the community can be reconstructed in terms of its functions. The edifying tale of the original gathering of individuals placing their needs in common and exchanging their services (which political philosophy and its surrogates will drag around from age to age in naive or sophisticated versions) originally has this perfectly determined job of deconstructing and reconstructing appropriate to clearing the city of the demos, of its "freedom" and the places and times it is exercised. Before edifying the community about its own law, before the refounding gesture and the education of citizens, the way of life set up by the *politeia* is already there in embryo form in the

66

fable of the four workers who have to mind their own business.[2] The virtue of minding your own business is called *sôphrosunê*, which we are forced to translate as "temperance" or "moderation," words that mask the strictly logical relationship expressed by this lower-class "virtue" behind pallid images of controlling appetites. *Sôphrosunê* is the strict answer to the "liberty" of the demos. Liberty was the paradoxical *axia* of the people, the common entitlement that the demos arrogated "to itself."

Symmetrically, *sôphrosunê*, which is defined as the virtue of the artisans, is nothing more than common virtue. But this similarity between the particular and the common works the other way around to the "liberty" of the demos. In no way does it belong to those whose sole virtue it is. It is simply the domination of the less good by the best. The particular and common virtue of those of the mob is nothing more than their submission to the order according to which they are merely what they are and do merely what they do. The *sôphrosunê* of the artisans is identical to their "lack of time." It is their way of living the interiority of the city as radical exteriority.

The order of the *politeia* thus presupposes the lack of any vacuum, saturation of the space and time of the community. The rule of law is also the disappearance of what is consubstantial to the law's mode of being wherever politics exists: the exteriority of writing. The republic is that community in which the law (the *nomos*) exists as living logos: as the ethos (morality, ways of being, character) of the community and of each of its members; as the occupation of the workers; as the tune playing in everyone's heads and the movement spontaneously animating their bodies; as the spiritual nourishment *(trophè)* that automatically turns their minds toward a certain cast *(tropos)* of behavior and thought. The republic is a system of tropisms. The politics of the philosophers does not begin, as the righteous would have us believe, with the law. It begins with the spirit of the law. That laws in the first instance express a community's way of being, temperament, climate, is not something some curious spirit of the Enlightenment suddenly stumbled upon. Or rather, if Montesquieu did stumble on such a spirit, in his own way, this is because it was already harnessed to the law in the original philosophical determination of political law. The equality of the law is first the equality of a mood. The good city is one in which the order of the *cosmos,* the geometric order that rules the movement of the divine stars, manifests itself as the temperament of a social body, in which the citizen acts not according to the law but according to the spirit of the law, the vital breath that gives it life. It is a city in which the citizen is won over by a story rather than restrained by a law, in which the legislator writing the laws is able to tightly work into them the admonitions necessary to citizens as well as "his opinion of what is beautiful and what is ugly."[3] It is a city in which legislation is entirely resumed in education — education, however, going beyond the simple instruction of the schoolmaster and being offered at any moment of the day in the chorus of what is visually and aurally up for grabs. Archipolitics is the complete achievement of *phusis* as *nomos,* community law's complete and tangible coming into being. There can be no time out, no empty space in the fabric of the community.

So such an archipolitics is just as much a form of archipolicing that grants ways of being and ways of doing, ways of feeling and ways of thinking, with nothing left over. But it would be reducing the scope of such archipolitics or archipolicing, as well as misunderstanding its legacy, if we were to confuse it with the philosopher's utopia or the fanaticism of the closed city. What Plato invents is broader and more durable: the opposition between republic and democracy. Plato substitutes the republic for democracy's regime of wrong and division, for the exteriority of a law that measures the effectiveness of the part of those who have no part in the conflict of parties. This republic is not so much based on law as a universal as on the education that constantly translates the law into its spirit. Plato invents the regime of community interiority in which the law is the harmony of the ethos, the accord between the *character* of individuals and the *moral values* of the collective. He invents the sciences that go with this internalization of the bond of community, those sciences of the individual and collective soul that modernity will call psychology and sociology. The "republican" project, as it

68

is elaborated in Plato's archipolitics, is the complete psychologizing and sociologizing of the elements of the political apparatus. In place of the disturbing elements of political subjectification, the *politeia* puts the roles, aptitudes, and feelings of the community conceived as a body animated by the one soul of the whole: distribution of trades, unity of ethical tropisms, unison of fables and refrains.

It is important to see how the idea of a republic, the project of education, and the invention of the sciences of the individual and collective soul hold together as features of the archipolitical apparatus. The "resurrection" of political philosophy proclaimed today arises as a reaction to the illegitimate encroachment of the social sciences on the domain of politics and on the prerogatives of political philosophy. The ideal of the republic and its universalist instruction also happily contrasts with a school system subject to the parasitical imperatives of a kind of psychopedagogy and sociopedagogy, linked to the twin derailments of democratic individualism and totalitarian socialism. But such polemics generally overlook the fact that it was "political philosophy" that invented the "liberal and social" sciences as community sciences. The centrality of *paideia* in the republic also means the primacy of harmonizing individual personality and collective morality throughout the entire distribution of knowledge. The republic of Jules Ferry, a paradise supposedly lost of the universalism of the citizen, was born in the shadows of the liberal and social sciences, which were themselves a legacy of the archipolitical project. The school system and the republic have not just recently been perverted by psychology and sociology. They have merely changed brands of psychology and sociology, and changed the way teachings about the individual and collective soul work within the system of knowledge distribution, redistributed the relationship of pedagogical mastery, the anarchy of the democratic circulation of knowledge and the republican development of harmony between personality and morality. They have not abandoned the universal for the particular; they have simply combined the singularized (polemical) universal of democracy and the particularized (ethical) universal of the republic in a different way. Philosophical and republican denunciations of

69

sociological imperialism, like sociological denunciations of a philosophy and a republic that denigrate the laws of social and cultural reproduction, equally overlook the initial nexus established by archipolitics between a community based on the proportions of the cosmos and the work of the sciences of the individual and collective soul.

Archipolitics, as formulated by Plato, thus amounts to full achievement of *phusis* as *nomos*—which presupposes eliminating certain elements of the polemical apparatus of politics and replacing them with community law's various forms of sensitization or consciousness-raising. Replacing an empty qualification (the *freedom* of the people) with an equally empty virtue (the *sôphrosunê* of the artisans) is the pivotal point of such a process. The result is the total elimination of politics as a specific activity. But parapolitics, basically invented by Aristotle, refuses to pay this price. Like any other "political philosophy," it tends, ultimately, to identify political activity with the police order, but does so from the point of view of the specificity of politics. The specificity of politics is disruption, the effect of equality as the litigious "freedom" of the people. It is the original division of *phusis* that is called on to be achieved as community *nomos*. There is politics because equality comes along and carries out this original split in the "nature" of politics, which is the condition for even being able to imagine the "nature" of politics. Aristotle tackles this split, this submission of the community telos to the fact of equality, at the beginning of the second book of *Politics*, the one where he settles his score with Plato. No doubt, says Aristotle, it would be better if the most virtuous were to rule over the city and if they were to rule forever. But this natural order of things is impossible wherever you have a city where "all are by nature equal."[4] No point asking what makes such an equality natural or why it is natural in Athens but not in Lacedaemonia: it suffices that it exists. In such a city, and whether this is a good or a bad thing, it is *just* that all share in ruling and that this equal share manifest itself in a specific "imitation": the alternation between the place of the ruler and the place of the ruled.

Everything hinges on these few lines that separate the good proper to politics — justice — from all other forms of good. The good of politics begins by dismantling the simple tautology according to which what is good is that the best prevail over the less good. Once equality exists and coalesces as the freedom of the people, what is *just* can never be synonymous with what is *good* and deployment of the goodness tautology. The virtue of the good man, which is to rule, is not the virtue proper to politics. Politics exists only because there are equals and it is over them that rule is exercised. The problem is not just having to "put up with" the plain fact of the dubious freedom of the demos, for this plain fact is also the fact of politics, that which distinguishes politics' own *arkhê* from all other forms of rule. The rest are all exercised by a superior over an inferior. Changing the mode of this superiority, as Socrates suggests to Thrasymachus, is completely pointless. If politics means anything, it is only on the basis of a perfectly peculiar capacity simply unimaginable before the existence of the demos: the equal capacity to rule and be ruled. This virtue cannot be reduced to that old military virtue of training people to rule through the practice of obedience. Plato gave space to such apprenticeship through obedience, but obedience is still not the political capability of permutability — of changing places. Thus Plato's city is not political. But a nonpolitical city is no city at all. Plato makes up a strange monster that imposes the mode of rule of the family on the city. That Plato needs to eliminate the family in order to do so is a perfectly logical paradox: eliminating the difference between one and the other means eliminating them both. The only city is a political one and politics begins with egalitarian contingency.

The problem for parapolitics will be to reconcile the two concepts of nature and their opposing logics: the one in which the greatest good is the rule of the best and the other, in which the greatest good in terms of equality is equality. Whatever we may say about the Ancients and their city of common good, Aristotle effects a decisive break within this common good, thereby initiating a new brand of "political philosophy." That this new brand comes to be identified with the quintessence of political philosophy and that Aristotle is always the last resort of all its "restorers" is not too hard to understand. Aristotle in effect offers the endlessly fascinating figure of an easy embodiment of the contradiction implied in the very term. It is Aristotle who managed to square the circle, to propose the realization of a natural order of politics as a constitutional order by the very inclusion of what blocked any such realization: the demos, either in the form of exposure of the war between the "rich" and the "poor," or in the ultimate form of the effectiveness of an egalitarian anarchy. He also manages the incredible feat of presenting this tour de force as the perfectly logical outcome of the original determination of the political animal. Just as Plato instantly pulls off the telos of an archipolitics that will function as the normal regime, so Aristotle instantly accomplishes the telos of a parapolitics that will function as the normal, honest regime of "political philosophy": transforming the actors and forms of action of the political conflict into the parts and forms of distribution of the policing apparatus.

So instead of replacing one order with another, parapolitics gets them to overlap. The demos, through which the specificity of politics occurs, becomes one of the parties to a political conflict that is identified with conflict over the occupation of "offices," the *arkhaï* of the city. This is why Aristotle pins down "political philosophy" to a center that will afterward appear quite natural even though it is no such thing. This center is the institutional apparatus of the *arkhaï* and the relationship of mastery played out in it, what the moderns will call power and for which Aristotle has no noun, only an adjective — *kurion*, the dominant element, the one who, by exercising dominion over others, gives the community its dominant characteristic, its own style. Parapolitics is, first, this centering of political thought on the place and mode of allocation of the *arkhaï* by which a regime defines itself in exercising a certain *kurion*. Such centering seems obvious to a modernity for whom the issue of politics is quite naturally one of power, of the principles that legitimize power, the forms in which power is distributed, and the types of personality specific to it. But it is important for us to see that it is a peculiar response to the specific paradox of politics, to the confrontation between the police logic of the distribution of parts and the political logic of the part of those who have no part. Aristotle shifts the peculiar tying in of the effect of equality and the inegalitarian logic of social bodies that is the stuff of politics toward a *single* politics as the specific place of institutions. The conflict between the two logics thereby becomes the conflict between the two parties struggling to occupy the *arkhaï* and to conquer the *kurion* of the city. In a word, the theoretical paradox of politics, the meeting of incommensurables, becomes the practical paradox of government. This takes the form of a thorny problem, certainly, but one that can be rigorously formulated as the relationship between homogenous givens: government of the city, the authority that directs and maintains it, is always government by one of the "parties," one of the factions that, by imposing its law on the other, imposes on the city the law of division. The problem is therefore how to work it so that the city is preserved by a "government" whose logic, whatever it may be, is domination of the other party who is responsible for keeping up the dissension that destroys the city.

The Aristotelian solution, as we know, is to turn the problem around. Since any government, through its own natural law, creates the sedition that will overthrow it, each government ought to go against its own law. Or rather, it ought to discover its true law, the law common to all governments: such a law urges it to keep going and to go against the grain in order to do so, using whatever means may ensure the safeguarding of all governments and with it, the city they govern. The tendency proper to tyranny is to serve the interests and pleasure of the tyrant alone, which incites the combined revolt of the oligarchs and the masses and so brings about the imbalance that causes tyranny to topple. The sole means of preserving tyranny will thus be for the tyrant to submit to the rule of law and to promote the material betterment of the people and the participation in power of men of substance. Oligarchs habitually swear among themselves to thwart the people in every way, and they keep their word consistently enough to attract the inevitable popular uprising that will destroy their power. If only, on the contrary, they applied themselves to serving the interests of the people at all times, their power would be shored up. They ought to apply themselves accordingly— or at least look as though they are. For politics is a question of aesthetics, a matter of appearances. The good regime is one that takes on the appearances of an oligarchy for the oligarchs and democracy for the demos. Thus the party of the rich and the party of the poor will be brought to engage in the same "politics," that politics nowhere to be found of those who are neither rich nor poor, that middle class everywhere missing, not only because the restricted framework of the city gives it no space to develop but, more profoundly, because politics is the business of rich and poor alone. The social thus remains the utopia of politics policed, and through a sleight of hand in the redistribution of powers and the appearances of power each *politeia*, each form of— bad— government, approaches its homonym, the *politeia*, the government of law. For the law to rule, every regime, in order to preserve itself, must cancel itself out in that intermediate regime that is the ideal regime of apportionment, at least when democracy has already laid the groundwork.

According to his new archetype, the philosopher, as sage and artist, lawmaker and reformer, rearranges the components of the democratic apparatus (the appearance of the people, its unequal count, and its founding dispute) into the forms of rationality of the good government that achieves the telos of the community in the distribution of powers and their modes of visibility. Through a singular mimesis, the demos and its miscount— preconditions for politics— are integrated in the achievement of the telos of the nature of the community. But this integration only attains perfection in the form of a *mise en absence,* a withdrawal of presence. This is what is expressed in the famous hierarchy of types of democracy presented in books IV and VI of *Politics.* The best democracy is a peasant democracy, for it is precisely the one in which the demos is missing from its place. The dispersal of peasants— "the farming element" — in distant fields and the constraint of labor prevent them from going and occupying *their* place of power. They may bear the title of sovereignty, but they leave its concrete exercise to the wellborn. The law then rules, says Aristotle, through lack of resources:[5] lack of money and time off for going to the assembly, lack of the means that would enable the demos to be an effective mode of political subjectification. The community then contains the demos without suffering from its conflict. The *politeia* is thus realized as the distribution of bodies over a territory that keeps them apart from each other, leaving the central space of politics to the "better off" alone. There are two peoples, each marked by their own difference; one people's internal difference mimics and cancels out the other's. The spatialization — the internal difference of the properly constituted demos — turns round by mimicking the internal difference of the democratic people. This utopia of democracy corrected, of spatialized politics, will prove to be very durable, too: Tocqueville's "good" democracy, that America of wide open spaces where you do not meet a soul, is a reflection of it, as is the Europe of our politicians, if a pale one. If Plato's archipolitics is transposed in the modern age into the sociology of the social bond and common beliefs correcting democracy's sloppiness and giving coherence to the republican body, parapolitics gleefully transforms itself into another brand of "sociology": the representation of a democracy divided from itself, making a virtue, conversely, of the dispersal that prevents the people from forming. Plato's "political philosophy" and its substitutes propose to heal politics by substituting the truth of a social body animated by the soul of state functions for the litigious appearances of the demos, whereas Aristotle's political philosophy and its substitutes propose attainment of the idea of good through exact mimesis of the democratic discord blocking its attainment: the ultimate utopia of a sociologized politics, flipped over to its reverse, the serene end of politics whereby both senses of "end," as a telos fulfilling itself and as an eliminating gesture, come to coincide exactly.

But before "political philosophy" thus gets transformed into "social science," the parapolitical enterprise takes on a modern form, one that can be summed up in the terms of "sovereign power" and "the social contract." It was Thomas Hobbes who hit on the formula and deployed it to attack the "political philosophy" of the Ancients. For Hobbes, the

Ancients' position is utopic in its assertion that human beings are by nature cut out for the polity and seditious in making a natural bent for politics the norm by which the first person who comes along can presume to judge whether a regime conforms to such an underlying polity and to the good government that is its ideal accomplishment. Hobbes is among the first to perceive the singular nexus of politics and political philosophy. The concepts that political philosophy borrows from politics to elaborate the rules of a community where there is no dispute are endlessly reclaimed by politics to work up a new dispute. Aristotle thus sorted out regimes into good and bad according to whether they served the interests of all or the interests of the sovereign party. The tyrant distinguishes himself from the king not through the form his power takes but in its finality. By changing the tools of his tyranny, the tyrant behaves "as though" he were changing its ends.[6] He turns his tyranny into a quasi-monarchy as a means of serving his own interests and those of the community at the same time. The gap between the two terms is only mentioned to show the possibility of things turning out the same: a good tyrant is like a king and it hardly matters what you call him after that. Hobbes is faced with the reversal of this relationship: the name "tyrant" is an empty term that allows any old preacher, officer, or man of letters to contest the conformity of the exercise of royal power with the ends of royalty, to judge that a tyrant is a bad king. A bad king is a tyrant. And a tyrant is a false king, someone who holds the place of the king illegitimately, whom it is therefore legitimate to drive off or kill. Similarly, Aristotle kept the name "people" by emphasizing the gap between the name of the sovereign people and the reality of the power of men of substance. Here, too, things are reversed: the empty name of people becomes the subjective power of judging the gap between royalty and its essence and of putting this judgment into effect by reopening the dispute. The problem is then to eliminate this floating count of the people that stages the distance of a regime from its norm. The truly calamitous evil, says Hobbes, is that "private persons"[7] take it upon themselves to decide what is just and unjust. But what Hobbes understands by "private persons" is nothing other than those who, in Aristotelian terms, "have no part" in the government of the common sphere. What is at stake is thus the very structure of the wrong that institutes politics, the effectiveness of equality as the part of those who have no part, the definition of "parties" who are in fact the subjects of the dispute. To nip the evil in the bud and disarm "the false opinions of the vulgar touching on right and wrong,"[8] one must refute the very idea of some kind of natural political aptitude in the human animal that would predestine them to any good other than simple survival. One must establish that an aptitude for politics only comes second, that it is only the triumph of a sense of survival over limitless desire that pits all against all.

The paradox is that, in order to refute Aristotle, all Hobbes basically does is shift Aristotle's reasoning—the triumph of the reasonable desire for survival over the passions peculiar to the democrat, the oligarch, and the tyrant. He shifts Aristotle's reasoning from the level of the "parties" in power to the level of individuals, from a theory of government to a theory about the origins of power. This double shift, which creates a privileged object for modern political philosophy, the origins of power, has a most specific purpose: it at once annihilates the part of those who have no part. A bent for politics thus exists only through an initial and total alienation of a freedom that belongs only to individuals. Freedom cannot exist as the part of those who have no part, as the empty property of any political subject. It has to be all or nothing. It can only exist in two forms: as a property of purely asocial individuals or in its state of radical alienation as the sovereignty of the sovereign.

This also means that sovereignty is no longer domination of one party over another. It is the radical "dismissal of the case" of the parties and of what their interplay gives rise to: the effectiveness of the part of those who have no part. The problematization of the "origins" of power and the terms in which it is framed—the social contract, alienation, and sovereignty—declare first that there is no part of those who have no part. There are only individuals and the power of the state. Any party putting right and wrong at stake contradicts the very concept of a community. Rousseau attacked the frivolity of Hobbes's demonstration. To refute the idea of natural sociability by invoking catty salon gossip and court intrigues is a crude *hysteron proteron*. But Rousseau — and the modern republican tradition after him — is in agreement about the serious stakes of this frivolous demonstration: the eradication of the part of those who have no part that Aristotelian theory determinedly integrated into its very negation. Rousseau is in agreement with the Hobbesian tautology of sovereignty: sovereignty rests solely on itself, for beyond it there are only individuals. All other bodies in the game of politics are merely factions. Modern parapolitics begins by inventing a specific nature, an "individuality," strictly correlating to the absolute of a sovereign power that must exclude quarreling between fractions, quarreling between parts and parties. It begins by initially breaking down the people into individuals, which, in one go, exorcises the class war of which politics consists, in the war of all against all. Supporters of the "Ancients" are only too happy to see the origin of the disasters of modern politics in the fatal substitution of "subjective rights" for the objective rule of law that was to have been the basis of the Aristotelian political "association." But Aristotle does not recognize "right" as an organizing principle of civilian and political society. He recognizes the *just* and its different forms. Now, for Aristotle, the political form the just takes is what determines the relationships between the "parts" of the community. Modernity not only places "subjective" rights in place of the objective rule of law; it invents right as the *philosophical* principle of the *political* community. This invention goes hand in hand with the myth of origins, the fable of the relationship of individuals to the whole, made to obliterate the litigious relationship between parts. Incidentally, *right* as conceptualized by "political philosophy" to settle the issue of wrong is one thing; the right that politics puts to work in its mechanisms for dealing with a wrong is another. For politics is not based on right but on wrong, and what differentiates a politics of the Moderns from a politics of the Ancients is a different structure of wrong. We should add here, though, that the political processing of wrong never ceases to borrow elements from "political philosophy" to build up new arguments and manifestations of dispute. This is why modern forms of wrong attach to the dispute on behalf of parts of the community the new dispute that relates each one to the whole of sovereignty.

For this is where the paradox lies: the fiction of origins on which social peace is supposed to be based will in the long run open up the gulf of a dispute more radical than that of the Ancients. To refuse to accept the class struggle as a secondary logic, a second "nature" instituting politics, to set up at the outset the division of nature as the passage from natural right to natural law, is to admit equality pure and simple as politics' ultimate principle. The fable of the war of all against all is as idiotic as all fables of origins. But behind this feeble tale of death and salvation, something more serious makes itself felt, the declaration of the ultimate secret of any social order, the pure and simple equality of anyone and everyone: there is no natural principle of domination by one person over another. The social order ultimately rests on the equality that is also its ruination. No "convention" can change this defect of "nature"—unless it involves the total and irremediable alienation of all "freedom" in which such equality might take effect. Equality and freedom must therefore be identified at the start and annihilated together. The absolutes of alienation and sovereignty are necessary because of equality, which also means they are only justifiable at the cost of *naming* equality as the basis and original gulf of the community order, as the sole reason for inequality. And against the backdrop of this now openly declared equality the elements of the new political dispute range themselves, the reasons for alienation and for the inalienable that will emerge as arguments for new forms of the class war.

For a start, freedom has become peculiar to *individuals* as such and, contrary to Hobbes's intention, the fable of alienation will give rise to the question of knowing whether and under what conditions individuals may alienate this freedom completely—in a word, it will give rise to the right of the individual as nonright of the state, the *entitlement* of anyone at all to question the state or to serve as proof of its infidelity to its own principle. On the other hand, the people, who were supposed to be eliminated in the tautology of sovereignty, will emerge as the entity that must be presupposed for alienation to be thinkable and finally as the real subject of sovereignty. Rousseau performs this demonstration in his critique of Grotius. The "liberty" of the people that had to be eradicated can then make a comeback as being identical to the achievement of the common power of men born "free and equal in law." It can then be argued for in the structure of a radical wrong, the wrong done to those men "born free and everywhere in chains." Aristotle had already acknowledged the accidental fact of those cities where the poor are "free by nature" and the paradox linking their "accidental" nature to the very definition of the nature of politics. But the myth of origins, in its final transformation, absolutizes the dispute of the proper and improper freedom of the people into the original contradiction of a freedom that each subject — each man — originally possesses and is dispossessed of. Man is then the subject itself of the relationship between all and nothing, the dizzying short circuit between the world of beings who are born and die and the terms of equality and freedom. And *right*, whose philosophical determination was produced to put paid to the nexus between *justice* and dispute, becomes the new name, the name par excellence, for wrong. Behind all demonstrations of a count of the uncounted, behind all worlds of association organized to manifest a dispute, the key figure of he whose count is always in deficit will from now on be found: this man who is not counted unless any one of his responses is also, but who is also never counted in his integrity if he is counted only as a political animal. In denouncing the compromise Aristotelian parapolitics makes with the sedition menacing the social body, and in breaking down the demos into individuals, the parapolitics of the social contract and of sovereign power opens up a more radical gap than the old political gap of the part taken for the whole. It sets out the distance of man from himself as the primary and final basis of the distance of the people from itself.

For at the same time the sovereign people shows up so does its namesake (which it in no way resembles): denial or derision of sovereignty, that prepolitical or beyond-political people known as the population or populace — a toiling, suffering population, the ignorant masses, the rabble, chained or unchained, whose existence undermines or contradicts the attainment of sovereignty. Hence the reopening of the gap in the modern people, this gap inscribed in the problematic conjunction of the terms man and the citizen: elements of a new apparatus of political dispute whereby each term serves to reveal the noncount of the other, but also the basis for reopening the gap between archipolitics and politics and setting up this gap on the very stage of politics. The political effectiveness of this archipolitical gap has a name. That name is terror. Terror is the political *agir* that adopts as its *political* task the requirement of achieving community *arkhê*, its internalization and promotion of total awareness of it. This means terror adopts the archipolitical program but it does so in the terms of modern parapolitics, those of the exclusive relationship between the sovereign power and individuals who, each on their own behalf, spell the virtual dissolution of that sovereign power, in themselves threatening the citizenship that is the soul of the whole.

Against the backdrop of radical wrong — the inhumanity of man — will thus intersect the new wrong that connects individuals and their rights to the state; the wrong that leaves the real sovereign — the people — grappling with the usurpers of sovereignty; the discrepancy between the sovereign people and the people as a party; the wrong that pits classes against each other and the wrong that pits the reality of their conflicts against the interplay of the individual and the state. It is in this interplay that the third great archetype of the "politics of the philosophers" is forged. It will be known as metapolitics. Metapolitics is situated symmetrically in relation to archipolitics. Archipolitics revoked false politics, that is, democracy. It declared a radical gap between real justice, resembling divine proportion, and democratic stagings of wrong, assimilated to the reign of injustice. Symmetrically, metapolitics declares a radical surplus of injustice or inequality in relation to what politics puts forward as justice or equality. It asserts absolute wrong, the surplus of wrong that destroys any political deployment of the argument of equality. In terms of this surplus it, too, reveals one of the "truths" of politics. But this truth is of a particular kind. It is not some idea of good, justice, the divine *cosmos* or true equality that would allow

81

a real community to be set up in place of the political lie. The truth of politics is the manifestation of its falseness. It is the gap between any political process of naming or inscribing in relation to the realities subtending them.

No doubt such a reality can be named, and metapolitics will call it the social, social issues, social classes, the real movement of society. But the social is not the reality of politics except at the cost of being the reality of its falseness: not so much the sensitive stuff of which politics is made as the name of its radical falseness. In the modern "political philosophy" apparatus, the truth of politics is no longer located above politics as its essence or idea. It is located beneath or behind it, in what it conceals and exists only to conceal. Metapolitics is the exercise of this particular truth, one no longer found facing democratic factuality as the good model confronting the fatal simulacrum, but as the secret of life and death, coiled at the very heart of any manifestation of politics. Metapolitics is the discourse on the falseness of politics that splits every political manifestation of dispute, in order to prove its ignorance of its own truth by marking, every time, the gap between names and things, the gap between enunciation of some logos of the people, of man or of the citizenry and the account that is made of this, the gap that reveals a fundamental injustice, itself identical with a constitutive lie. If the archipolitics of antiquity proposed a medicine of community health, modern metapolitics presents itself as a symptomology that detects a sign of untruth within every political distinction — that between man and the citizen, for instance.

Clearly it was Marx who provided the canonical formula for metapolitical interpretation, especially in *The Jewish Question*. The target is exactly the same as for Plato, that is, democracy as the perfecting of a certain politics — in other words, the perfection of its lie. The basis for calling it into question is strictly provided by the gap between an ideal identified by a Rousseauist figuration of the sovereignty of citizenship and a reality conceived in Hobbesian terms as the war of all against all. The processing of this gap between Hobbesian man and Rousseauist citizen undergoes a significant inflection in the course of Marx's text.

At first the gap signifies the limits of politics, its powerlessness to achieve the properly human part of man. Man's emancipation is then the truth of free humanity outside the limits of political citizenship. But, along the way, this truth about man trades places. Man is not some future accomplishment beyond political representation. He is the truth hidden beneath this representation: man of civil society, the egotistical property owner matched by the non–property owner whose rights as a citizen are only there to mask radical nonright. The inability of citizenship to achieve man's true humanity becomes its capacity to serve, by masking them, the interests of man the property owner. Political "participation" is then just the mask of the allocation of lots. Politics is the lie about a reality that is called society. But, by the same token, the social is always ultimately reducible to the simple untruth of politics.

The social as the truth of politics is caught in a great divide. On one side, it can be the "realistic" and "scientific" name of "man's humanity." The movement of production and that of the class struggle then become the true movement that should, through its achievement, dispel the appearances of political citizenship in favor of the reality of productive man. But this positivity is at once eroded by the ambiguity of the concept of class. *Class* is the perfect example of one of those homonyms over which the counts of the police order and those of the political demonstration are divided. In the police sense, a class is a grouping of people assigned a particular status and rank according to their origins or their activity; in this sense, class may denote a professional group in the weaker sense. One thus speaks, in the nineteenth century, of the class of printers or the class of hatters. In the stronger sense, class is synonymous with caste. Whence the apparent paradox whereby those who are counted without any problem in the count of the working class*es* more often than not refuse to recognize the existence of *a* working class constituting a division of society and giving them a specific identity. In the political sense, a *class* is something else entirely: an operator of conflict, a name for counting the uncounted, a mode of subjectification superimposed on the reality of all social groups. The Athenian demos or the proletariat, in whose ranks the "bourgeois" Blanqui counts himself, are classes of this kind, that is, forces for declassifying social species, those "classes" that bear the same name as they do. Now, in between these two rigorously opposed kinds of class, Marxist metapolitics introduces an ambiguity in which all the philosophical *disagreement* about political *disagreement* is concentrated.

The latter may be summed up in the definition of the proletariat: "a class in society that is *no longer* a class in society," says the *Introduction to the Critique of Hegel's Philosophy of Right*. The problem is that in these words, Marx only gives a rigorous definition of what a class is in the political sense, that is, in terms of the class struggle. The term *proletariat* is just the name of the uncounted, a mode of subjectification that places the part of those who have no part in a new dispute. Marx in a way renames the "classes" that the fiction of man and of sovereignty tries to do away with, but he renames them paradoxically. He renames them as the infrapolitical truth in which the political lie is made to collapse. He conceives of the ordinary exceptionality of that class that is a nonclass as the outcome of a process of social disintegration. In a word, Marx turns a political category into the concept of the untruth of politics. From then on, the concept of class begins to oscillate indefinitely and the meaning of metapolitics with it between a radicalism of "true" politics, symmetrical to that of Platonic archipolitics, and a nihilism of the falseness of all politics that is also the political nihilism of the falseness of all things.

In one sense, the concept of class is accepted as the *truth* of the political lie. But this truth itself oscillates between two extreme poles. On the one hand, it has the positive force of a social content. The class struggle is the true movement of society, and the proletariat, or the working class, is the social force driving this movement to the point where its truth causes the illusion of politics to explode. Thus defined, the working class and the proletariat are positive social forces and their "truth" lends itself to supporting all ethical embodiments of the productive working people. But, at the other extreme, they are defined by their sole negativity as "nonclasses." They are mere performers of revolutionary acts by which measure any form of democratic subjectification, as well as any positive social grouping, seems radically deficient. These two extreme poles strictly define two extremisms: an infrapolitical extremism of class, that is, of the social embodiment of political classes, and an ultrapolitical extremism of nonclass—opposing extremisms whose homonyms, class and nonclass, allow them to come together in the single figure of the terrorist.

As the *truth* of the lie of politics, the concept of class thus becomes the central figure of a metapolitics conceived as a *beyond* of politics, in keeping with one of the two senses of the prefix. But metapolitics can be understood at the same time according to the other sense of the prefix, which indicates *a complement, an accompaniment.* So metapolitics becomes the scientific accompaniment of politics, in which the reduction of political forms to the forces of the class struggle is initially equivalent to the *truth of the lie* or the truth of illusion. But it also becomes a "political" accompaniment of all forms of subjectification, which posits as its hidden "political" truth the class struggle it underestimates and cannot not underestimate. Metapolitics can seize on any phenomenon as a demonstration of the truth of its falseness. For the truth of falseness, Marx in his genius invented a key word that all modernity has adopted, at times even turning it against him. He called it *ideology.* Ideology is not just a new word for simulacrum or illusion. Ideology is the word that signals the completely new status of the true that metapolitics forges: the true as the truth of the false. Not the clarity of the idea in the face of the obscurity of appearances; not the truth as an index of itself and of falseness but, on the contrary, the truth of which the false alone is an index, the truth that is nothing more than highlighting falseness, the truth as universal interference. Ideology is thus something else entirely from a new name for an old idea. In inventing it, Marx invents, for a time that is still with us, an unheard-of regime of truth and a completely new connection between truth and politics. Ideology is a name for the endlessly decried gap between words and things, the conceptual connector that organizes the junctions and disjunctions between the components of the modern political apparatus. It alternately allows the political appearance of the people to be reduced to the level of an illusion concealing the reality of conflict or, conversely, the names of the people and the manifestations of its dispute to be put down as outdated, holding up the emergence of common interests. Ideology is the term that links the production of politics to its evacuation, that designates the distance between words and things as the falseness in politics that can always be turned into the falseness of politics. But it is also the concept by means of which anything is declared to stem from politics, to arise from a "political" demonstration of its falseness. It is, in short, the concept in which all politics is canceled out, either through its proclaimed evanescence, or, on the contrary, through the assertion that everything is political, which comes down to saying that nothing is, that politics is only the parasitical mode of truth. Ideology is, finally, the term that allows the place of politics to shift endlessly, right to the dizzy limit: the declaration of its end. What in police language is called "the end of politics" is perhaps nothing more, in fact, than completion of the process whereby metapolitics, inextricably bound up with politics and binding everything together as "political," evacuates it from the inside, causing the constitutive wrong of politics to disappear in the name of the critique of all appearance. At the end of the process, wrong, having been through the wringer of its own absolutization, is reduced to infinite reiteration of the truth of falseness, to mere demonstration of an empty truth. The politics it once founded can then be identified with that original paradise, nowhere to be found, where individuals and groups use the faculty of speech unique to man in order to reconcile their particular interests in the reign of the general interest. The end of politics declared at the grave of police Marxisms is, in short, only the other form, the "liberal" capitalist form, of Marxist metapolitics. The "end of politics" is the ultimate phase of metapolitical interference, the final affirmation of the emptiness of its truth. The "end of politics" is the completion of political philosophy.

More precisely, the "end of politics" is the end of the strained relationship between politics and metapolitics that has characterized the age of modern democratic and social revolutions. This strained relationship has been played out in interpretations of the difference between man and the citizen, the suffering-working people and the sovereign people. There are in effect two main ways of conceiving and dealing with this gap. The first is the one metapolitics takes whereby the gap is seen as denunciation of an impossible identification, the sign of the untruth of the ideal sovereign people. Metapolitics defines as formal democracy the system of juridical inscriptions and government institutions based on the concept of the sovereignty of the people. So characterized, "form" finds itself opposed to a virtual or missing content, to the reality of a power that really would belong to the popular community. From that moment, its meaning may vary, from the simple illusion masking the reality of power and dispossession to the necessary mode of presenting a social contradiction not yet sufficiently developed. In any case, the metapolitical interpretation of the internal division of the people divides any political scene in two: there are those who play the game of forms (the vindication of rights, the battle for representation, etc.) and those who direct the action designed to eradicate this play of forms. On the one hand, the people of legal and political representation; on the other, the people of the social and workers' movement, performers in the true movement that eliminates the political appearances of democracy.

This metapolitical version of the gap between man and the citizen, between the laboring people and the sovereign people, is opposed by the political version. For politics, the fact that the people are internally divided is not, actually, a scandal to be deplored. It is the primary condition of the exercise of politics. There is politics from the moment there exists the sphere of appearance of a subject, *the people,* whose particular attribute is to be different from itself, internally divided. So, from the political point of view, the inscriptions of equality that figure in the Declaration of the Rights of Man or the preambles to the Codes and Constitutions, those that symbolize such and such an institution or are engraved on the pediments of their edifices, are not "forms" belied by their contents or "appearances" made to conceal reality. They are an effective mode of appearance of the people, the minimum of equality that is inscribed in the field of common experience. The problem is not to accentuate the difference between this existing equality and all that belies it. It is not to contradict appearances but, on the contrary, to confirm them. Wherever the part of those who have no part is inscribed, however fragile and fleeting these inscriptions may be, a sphere of appearance of the demos is created, an element of the *kratos*, the power of the people, exists. The problem is to extend the sphere of this materialization, to maximize this power.

Maximizing this power means creating litigious cases and worlds of community in litigation by demonstrating the difference of the people from itself under whatever specifications. There is not on the one hand the ideal people of the founding texts and, on the other, the real people of the workshops and suburbs. There is a place where the power of the people is inscribed and places where this power is reputedly ineffective. The space of work or domestic space does not contradict the power inscribed in the texts. To contradict this, they would first of all have to confirm it, they would have to be concerned by it. But according to police logic, no one can *see* how or why they would be. So the problem is to construct a visible relationship with the nonrelationship, an effect of a supposedly ineffective power. And so it is no longer a matter of interpreting the difference between one people and another according to some kind of symptomology. It is a matter of interpreting, in the theatrical sense of the word, the gap between a place where the demos exists and a place where it does not, where there are only populations, individuals, employers and employees, heads of households and spouses, and so on. Politics consists in interpreting this relationship, which means first setting it up as theater, inventing the argument, in the double logical and dramatic sense of the term, connecting the unconnected. This invention is neither the feat of the sovereign people and its "representatives" nor the feat of the nonpeople/people of labor and their sudden "awareness."

It is the work of what we might call a third people, operating as such or under some other name and tying a particular dispute together on behalf of the uncounted. *Proletarian* has been the privileged name under which this liaison has been performed. In other words, the name of "that class that is not one," which served in metapolitics as the very name of the truth of political illusion, has served in politics as one of those subject names that organize a dispute: not the name of some universal victim, but rather the name of a universalizing subject of wrong. It has served as the name of a mode of political subjectification. In politics, subjects do not have consistent bodies; they are fluctuating performers who have their moments, places, occurrences, and the peculiar role of inventing *arguments* and *demonstrations*—in the double, logical and aesthetic, senses of the terms—to bring the nonrelationship into relationship and give place to the nonplace. This invention is performed in forms that are not metapolitical "forms" of a problematic "content," but forms of materialization of the people, which oppose metapolitical "appearances." Similarly, "right" is not the illusory attribute of an ideal subject; it is the arguing of a wrong. Since the declaration of equality exists somewhere, it is possible to affect its power, to organize its encounter with the ordinary ancestral distribution of bodies by posing the question, Is such and such a relationship included or not included in the sphere of manifestation of the equality of citizens? When French workers, at the time of the bourgeois monarchy, ask the question, "Are French workers French citizens?" (in other words, "Do they have the attributes recognized by Royal Charter as those of Frenchmen equal before the law?"), or when their feminist "sisters," at the time of the Republic, ask the question, "Are Frenchwomen included in the 'Frenchmen' who hold *universal* suffrage?," both workers and women are starting with the gap between the egalitarian inscription of the law and the spaces where inequality rules. But they in no way conclude from this that the case for the egalitarian text has been dismissed. On the contrary, they invent a new place for it: the polemical space of a demonstration that holds equality and its absence together. The demonstration, as we have seen, presents both the egalitarian text and the inegalitarian relationship at once. But also, through this very display, through the fact of addressing an interlocutor who does not acknowledge the interlocutory situation, it behaves as though it were being performed in a community whose nonexistence it at the same time demonstrates. Democratic politics opposes the metapolitical play of appearance and its denial with this practice of the *as if* that constitutes a subject's forms of materialization and that opens up an aesthetic community, in Kantian fashion, a community that demands the consent of the very person who does not acknowledge it.

Under the same names, the modern social and workers' movement thus presents the intertwining of two contrary logics. Its key word, proletarian, designates two very different "subjects." From the metapolitical point of view, it designates the performer of the real movement of society who denounces the democratic appearances of politics and is supposed to cause them to be blown to smithereens. For this reason, the declassifying class, the "dissolution of all classes," has become the subject of politics' reincorporation into the social. It has helped get off the ground the most radical figure of the archipolice order. From the political point of view, proletarian is a specific occurrence of the demos, a democratic subject, performing a demonstration of its power in the construction of worlds of litigious community, universalizing the issue of the count of the uncounted, beyond any regulation, short of infinite wrong. "Worker" and "prole" have thus been the names of actors in a double process: the actors of democratic politics, exposing and dealing with the internal division of the people, and metapolitical figures, actors in the "real movement" posited as dispelling political appearances and their crowning glory, the illusion of democracy. Metapolitics comes and wedges the relationship it creates between appearance and reality over all forms of dispute of the people. But the reverse is also true: to construct its arguments and manifestations, to connect the forms of visibility of the egalitarian logos with the places where it is invisible, the social and workers' movement has had to reconfigure the relationships between the visible and the invisible, relationships between ways of doing, ways of being, and ways of saying that operate on behalf of the workers and their words. But in order to do so, it has never ceased to take up those metapolitical arguments linking the just and the unjust to the interplay of "social" truth and "political" falseness. Metapolitics interpreted the forms of the democratic gap as symptoms of untruth. But it has not itself ceased being reinterpreted, offering matter and form for other ways of playing the gap and obliterating it.

The overall mechanism of these in-between interpretations has a name. It is called the *social*. If relations between the police and politics are determined by a few key words, a few major homonyms, we could say that, in modernity, the *social* has been the decisive homonym that has caused several logics and intertwinings of logics to connect and to disconnect, to oppose one another and to blur. The self-proclaimed "restorers" of politics and of "its" philosophy revel in the opposition of the political and a social seen to have unduly encroached on its prerogatives. But, in the modern era, the social has been precisely the place where politics has been played out, the very name it has taken on, wherever it has not simply been identified with the science of government and with the means of taking it over. This name is, it is true, similar to the name of its negation. But every politics works on homonyms and the indiscernable. Every politics also works on the verge of its radical demise, which is embodiment as the police, the realization of the political subject as social body. Political action always sticks to the in-between, between the "natural" figure, the police figure of the embodiment of a society carved up into functional organs and the borderline figure of some other archipolitical or metapolitical embodiment: the transformation of the subject that was useful in the disembodiment of the "natural" social body into a glorious corpus of truth. The age of the "social movement" and "social revolutions" has been an age in which the social has played every one of these roles. It has firstly been the police name for the distribution of groups and functions. Conversely, it has been the name in which mechanisms of political subjectification have come to contest the naturalness of such groups and functions by having the part of those who have no part counted. Finally, it has been the metapolitical name of a *true* politics that itself has taken two forms: the positive force of the real movement called upon to take shape as the principle behind a new social body, but also the sheer negativity of the interminable demonstration of the truth of falseness. The social has been the common name for all these logics as well as the name for their interlocking.

This also means that "social science," accused by some of having fraudulently introduced its empiricism into the rarefied atmosphere reserved for political philosophy, praised by others for having demystified the supposedly elevated concepts of such a philosophy, has been in fact the very form of existence political philosophy has taken in the age of democratic and social revolutions. Social science has been the final form taken by the strained relationship between philosophy and politics and by the philosophical project of achieving politics by doing away with it. This conflict and this project have been played out in the avatars of Marxist science or sociology à la Durkheim or à la Weber much more than in the supposedly pure forms of political philosophy. Marxist metapolitics defined the rules of the game: the shift between the real social body hidden beneath political appearances and endless assertion of the scientific truth of political falseness. Platonic archipolitics lent its model to the first age of the social sciences: that organic community defined by correct gearing of its functions under the government of the new religion of community. Aristotelian metapolitics provided the second age with its model of a community wisely placed at a distance from itself. The last age of sociology, which is also the final avatar of political philosophy, is a mere exposition of the rules of the game: the age of emptiness, it has been said, the age in which the truth of the social is reduced to that of the infinite interference of empty truth. Sociologists of this third age sometimes call this "the end of politics." Now perhaps we are at a point where we can understand: this "end of politics" is exactly the same as what the menders of "political philosophy" call "the return of politics." To return to pure politics and to the purity of "political philosophy" today has only one meaning. It means returning to a point this side of the conflict constitutive of modern politics as well as this side of the fundamental conflict between philosophy and politics: a theoretical idyll of a philosophical determination of the good that the political community would then have the task of achieving; a political idyll of achieving the common good by an enlightened government of elites buoyed by the confidence of the masses. The "philosophical" return of politics and its sociological "end" are one and the same.

Chapter 5

Democracy or Consensus

This idyllic state of politics generally goes by the name of consensus democracy. This chapter will try to show that this concept is, strictly speaking, the conjunction of contradictory terms. And so we propose the term "postdemocracy" to reflect on an object that is stranger than it looks. The term can only be justified by explaining some of the paradoxes inherent in the current dominant discourse on democracy.

Everywhere you turn the triumph of democracy is being trumpeted as a corollary to the collapse of so-called totalitarian systems. This triumph is supposed to be twofold. First, it is supposed to be the victory of democracy (understood as a political regime, a system of institutions causing popular sovereignty to materialize) over its adversary, proof that such a regime is both the most just and the most effective. The bankruptcy of so-called totalitarian states is in effect bankruptcy with regard to what was their ultimate legitimization: the argument of efficiency, of the system's ability to procure the material conditions of a new community. This then shores up legitimization of the so-called democratic regime: the idea that democracy ensures in one go political forms of justice and economic forms of production of wealth, as well as setting up interests and optimizing gains for all. But it is also, it

would seem, in its own eyes, a victory for democracy as a political practice. The history of the democratic movement in the West had been
haunted by democracy's persistent self-doubt. This was summed up in
the Marxist opposition between democracy on paper and real democracy, a metapolitical opposition often internalized in the very way political conflict was conducted. Democrats themselves have always remained
suspicious of democracy. Those who have fought most strenuously for
democratic rights have often been the first to suspect that these rights
were only theoretical, still a mere shadow of true democracy. Now, the
bankruptcy of the totalitarian system seems to finally raise the mortgage on a "real" democracy that maintained suspicion about democracy. It seems possible from that moment, and without any ulterior
motive, to enhance the standing of the forms of democracy (understood as the institutional mechanisms of the sovereignty of the people), to simply identify democracy with the legitimate state and liberalism and to see in democracy the ideal figure of the accomplishment
of the *phusis* of enterprising, desiring man as community *nomos*.

Democracy's success is gleefully attributed to the raising of a second mortgage, one that posited the idea of the people. Today democracy has given up posing as the power of the people. It has abandoned
the twin figure of the people that bogged politics down in the age of
modern revolutions: Rousseauist identification of the people with the
subject of sovereignty and Marxist—and more broadly, socialist—
identification with the worker as an empirical social figure and with
the proletarian or producer as the figure of a transcending of politics
in its truth. Indeed it has been said that this overdetermined people
was in the way of a truly political contract, one in which individuals
and groups come to agree on the right juridico-political forms to ensure the coexistence of all and the optimal participation of each one in
the community's fortunes.

This is, roughly, the schema of democracy's legitimization that functions as the balance sheet of the disaster of totalitarianism. But this
schema runs up against a paradox. Normally, the collapse of the "myths"
of the people and of "real" democracy should lead to the rehabilitation

of "formal" (theoretical) democracy, to increased attachment to the institutional mechanisms of the sovereignty of the people and principally to the forms of parliamentary control. But this is not what has happened at all. In the political system in France, for example, a continuous erosion of parliamentary representation can be observed, along with extension of the political powers of authorities who are not accountable (experts, judges, committees) and expansion of the sphere reserved for the president combined with a charismatic conception of the president's personality. The paradox is this: at the time the institutions of parliamentary representation were being contested, when the notion that these were "mere forms" held sway, they were nonetheless the object of a vastly superior militant vigilance. We have seen generations of militant socialists and communists battle fiercely for a constitution, rights, institutions, and institutional mechanisms that they otherwise claimed expressed the power of the bourgeoisie and of capital. Today the situation is the reverse and the victory of so-called formal democracy is accompanied by a noticeable disaffection with regard to its forms. Certainly, the zeitgeist offers its own response to the paradox. Apparently democratic wisdom would not consist in scrupulous attention to the institutions ensuring the power of the people through representative institutions so much as in the appropriateness of political practices to a society's ways of being, to the forces that move it, to the interlocking needs, interests, and desires from which the social fabric is woven. It would consist in appropriateness according to optimization theories that occur and overlap in the social body, and to the processes of individualization and to the solidarities these impose.

This response poses two problems. The first has to do with the way it chimes, curiously, with the argument of "real" democracy. At the very moment when Marxism's use-by date is being declared along with the failure of politics' bowing down to economics, we see regimes said to be liberal democracies take up, off their own bat, a sort of rampant Marxism according to which politics is the expression of a certain state of the social and it is the development of the forces of production that makes up the bulk of its forms. The declared success of democracy is then accompanied by a reduction of democracy to a certain state of social relationships. The success of democracy, in our societies, would then consist in its hitting on a coincidence between its political form and its tangible being.

But the paradox then takes another form. This identification of democracy with its tangible-being would indeed show itself in the privileged form of "disaffection," of insensitivity to the form of representation this tangible-being takes. Democracy would refer to a certain lived experience, a form of tangible experience, but a form of experience that is tangible rather than actually being felt: as though the only passion lay in lack, as though democracy—like love in the discourse of Lysias in Plato's *Phedra*—could only manage to have an impact at the cost of emptying itself of its own feeling. The problem is that lack always gets filled up and that, in our societies, the paradox of the disaffected form corresponds to a return, in unforeseeable form, of the people that had been interred. The people always, in fact, take shape at the very point they are declared finished. And, in place of the peoples Rousseau or Marx sent packing, there emerges here, there, and everywhere an ethnic people pinned down as identical to themselves, as one body set up against others.

At the heart of these paradoxes, then, lies the niggling question of democratic "forms" and of just what "form" might mean in this context. You would think the liberalism declared to reign shared the vision of Marxism, said to be defunct: a vision that conceptualizes the forms of politics in terms of the duality of form and content, political appearance and social reality; that defines the interplay of politics and the social as the relationship between a system of institutions and the movement of the energies of individuals and groups who would find themselves more or less adequately expressed in this system. Marxist metapolitics oscillated between a theory of form-expression and a theory of the appearance-mask. But the official discourse of triumphant democracy only rehabilitates "form" as disaffected form corresponding to an evanescent content, even if it means provoking a two-bit Platonism that once again pits the republican spirit of community against the small run-of-the-mill pleasures of democracy.

To find a way out of these debates, which in a way subcontract the remains of "political philosophy," we need to go back to its original stakes. Democracy initially stirred up political philosophy because it is not a set of institutions or one kind of regime among others but a way for politics to be. Democracy is not the parliamentary system or the legitimate State. It is not a state of the social either, the reign of individualism or of the masses. Democracy is, in general, politics' mode of subjectification if, by politics, we mean something other than the organization of bodies as a community and the management of places, powers, and functions. Democracy is more precisely the name of a singular disruption of this order of distribution of bodies as a community that we proposed to conceptualize in the broader concept of the police. It is the name of what comes and interrupts the smooth working of this order through a singular mechanism of subjectification.

This mechanism can be summed up in the three aspects already defined. First, democracy is the kind of community that is defined by the existence of a specific sphere of appearance of the people. Appearance is not an illusion that is opposed the real. It is the introduction of a visible into the field of experience, which then modifies the regime of the visible. It is not opposed to reality. It splits reality and reconfigures it as double. And so the first battle of "political philosophy" with democracy was Plato's polemic against the doxa, that is, the assimilation of the visible peculiar to the demos with the regime of untruth.

Second, the people occupying this sphere of appearance is a "people" of a particular kind, one not definable in terms of ethnic properties, one that does not identify with a sociologically determinable part of a population or with the sum of the groups that go to make up this population. The people through which democracy occurs is a unity that does not consist of any social group but that superimposes the effectiveness of a part of those who have no part on the reckoning of society's parties. Democracy is the designation of subjects that do not coincide with the parties of the state or of society, floating subjects that deregulate all representation of places and portions. One could no doubt evoke at this point Claude Lefort's conceptualization of democratic "indetermination,"[1] but there is really no reason to identify such indetermination with a sort of catastrophe in the symbolic linked to the revolutionary disembodiment of the "double body" of the king. We need to dissociate democratic disruption and disidentification from this theater of sacrifice that originally ties the emergence of democracy to the great specters of the reembodiments staged by terrorism and totalitarianism of a body torn asunder. And this duality is not the Christian duality of the celestial body and the earthly body: it is the duality of a social body and a body that now displaces any social identification.

Third, the place where the people appear is the place where a dispute is conducted. The political dispute is distinct from all conflicts of interest between constituted parties of the population, for it is a conflict over the very count of those parties. It is not a discussion between partners but an interlocution that undermines the very situation of interlocution. Democracy thus sets up communities of a specific kind, polemical communities that undermine the very opposition of the two logics — the police logic of the distribution of places and the political logic of the egalitarian act.

The forms of democracy are nothing other than the forms in which this ternary mechanism manifests itself. There is democracy if there is a specific sphere where the people appear. There is democracy if there are specific political performers who are neither agents of the state apparatus nor parts of society, if there are groups that displace identities as far as parts of the state or of society go. Lastly, there is democracy if there is a dispute conducted by a nonidentary subject on the stage where the people emerge. The forms of democracy are the forms taken by the emergence of this appearance, of such nonidentary subjectification and conducting of the dispute. These forms of emergence have an effect on the institutional mechanisms *of* politics and use whatever mechanisms they choose. They produce inscriptions of equality and they argue about existing inscriptions. And so they are in no way oblivious to the existence of elected assemblies, institutional guarantees of freedom of speech and expression, state control mechanisms. They see in these the conditions for being exercised and in turn modify them. But they do not identify with them. And still less can they be identified with individuals' ways of being.

Democracy is not the age of individuals or that of the masses. The correlation between a type of institution and a type of individuality is not something modern sociology stumbled upon: Plato, as we know, invented it. And it is clearly the archipolitical prescription of an affinity between the soul and the well-governed city that commands the description of an affinity between the nature of the democratic individual and that of their city. In other words, the idea of democracy as a regime of collective life expressing a *character*, a way of life of democratic individuals, itself belongs to the Platonic repression of democratic singularity, to the repression of politics itself. For the forms of democracy are nothing less than the forms in which politics is constituted as a specific mode of human being-together. Democracy is not a regime or a social way of life. It is the institution of politics itself, the system of forms of subjectification through which any order of distribution of bodies into functions corresponding to their "nature" and places corresponding to their functions is undermined, thrown back on its contingency. And, as we have seen, it is not their ethos, their "way of being," that disposes individuals to democracy but a break with this ethos, the gap experienced between the capability of the speaking being and any "ethical" harmony of doing, being, and saying. Every politics is democratic in this precise sense: not in the sense of a set of institutions, but in the sense of forms of expression that confront the logic of equality with the logic of the police order.

It is on this basis that we use the notion of postdemocracy here. This term should not be understood as the state of a democracy sadly surrendering its hopes or happily divested of its illusions. We should not look to it for a concept of democracy in the postmodern age. The term will simply be used to denote the paradox that, in the name of democracy, emphasizes the consensual practice of effacing the forms of democratic action. Postdemocracy is the government practice and conceptual legitimization of a democracy *after* the demos, a democracy that has eliminated the appearance, miscount, and dispute of the people and is thereby reducible to the sole interplay of state mechanisms and combinations of social energies and interests. Postdemocracy is not a democracy that has found the truth of institutional forms in the interplay of social energies. It is an identifying mode, among institutional mechanisms and the allocation of the society's appropriate parts and shares, for making the subject and democracy's own specific action disappear. It is the practice and theory of what is appropriate with nothing left over for forms of the state and the state of social relations.

This is the actual meaning of what is called consensus democracy. According to the reigning idyll, consensus democracy is a reasonable agreement between individuals and social groups who have understood that knowing what is possible and negotiating between partners are a way for each party to obtain the optimal share that the objective givens of the situation allow them to hope for and which is preferable to conflict. But for parties to opt for discussion rather than a fight, they must first exist as parties who then have to choose between two ways of obtaining their share. Before becoming a preference for peace over war, consensus is a certain regime of the perceptible: the regime in which the parties are presupposed as already given, their community established and the count of their speech identical to their linguistic performance. What consensus thus presupposes is the disappearance of any gap between a party to a dispute and a part of society. It is the disappearance of the mechanisms of appearance, of the miscount and the dispute opened up by the name "people" and the vacuum of their freedom. It is, in a word, the disappearance of politics. The ternary apparatus of democracy — that is, of politics — is strictly opposed by the proposition of a world in which everything is on show, in which parties are counted with none left over and in which everything can be resolved by objectifying problems. The so-called consensus system is the conjunction of a determined regime of *opinion* and a determined regime of *right*, both posited as regimes of the community's identification with itself, with nothing left over. As a regime of opinion, the principle of postdemocracy is to make the troubled and troubling appearance of the people and its always false count disappear behind procedures exhaustively presenting the people and its parts and bringing the count of those parts in line with the image of the whole. The utopia of postdemocracy is that of an uninterrupted count that presents the total of "public opinion" as identical to the body of the people. What in actual fact is this identification of democratic opinion with the system of polls and simulations? It is the absolute removal of the sphere of appearance of the people. In it the community is continually presented to itself. In it the people are never again uneven, uncountable, or unpresentable. They are always both totally present and totally absent at once. They are entirely caught in a structure of the visible where everything is on show and where there is thus no longer any place for appearance.

It is important to make this point clear by distancing ourselves from various analyses of simulation and the simulacrum, in particular those conducted by Jean Baudrillard. These have shown us a vast process of simulation involved in the complete and permanent exhibition of the real: everything is seen, nothing appears since everything is already there, identical to its representation, identical to the simulated production of its representation. The real and its simulation are then indistinguishable, which amounts to putting paid to a reality that no longer needs to happen, being always anticipated in its simulacrum. From that moment, this "loss of the real" can be interpreted in two different ways. The first emphasizes the complete conjuring trick that is the principle of equivalence of the real and its simulation.[2] The second gleefully salutes this loss of the real as the basis of a new politics.[3] According to this latter, the domination of media technology, reducing the world to a succession of images of it, delivered from the tyranny of truth, is a reversal of the technological domination that vaporizes metaphysics's world of objects inspected, weighed, and manipulated, and opens the way to an authentic emancipation of the multiple. Emancipation, in the Marxist era, was conceived in terms of work and history, in the concepts of metaphysics and its universe of manipulated objects. The new emancipation is supposed to be a reflection of the turnaround of technology and its destruction of metaphysics. It is supposed to liberate the new community as a multiplicity of local rationalities and ethnic, sexual, religious, cultural, or aesthetic minorities, affirming their identity on the basis of the acknowledged contingency of all identity.

These ways of conceptualizing the relationship between a certain status of the visible, an image of the world, and a form of political acting seem to miss a crucial point, which is that the logic of simulation does not so much oppose the real and realist faith as appearance and its powers. The regime of the all-visible, of the endless presentation to each and every one of us of a real indissociable from its image, is not the liberation of appearance. It is, on the contrary, its loss. The world of total visibility carves out a real where appearance has no place to occur or to produce its divisive, fragmenting effects. Appearance, particularly political appearance, does not conceal reality but in fact splinters it, introduces contentious objects into it, objects whose mode of presentation is not homogeneous with the ordinary mode of existence of the objects thereby identified. The identification of the real with its reproduction and simulation is the "dismissal of the case" for the heterogeneity of appearance, and with it, the dismissal of the case for the political constitution of nonidentary subjects that upsets the homogeneity of the perceptible by showing separate worlds together, by organizing worlds of litigious community. The "loss of the real" is in fact a loss of appearance. What it "liberates" is not some new politics of the contingent multiple, it is the police figure of a population exactly identical to the counting of its parts.

This is indeed what is set up by the conjunction of media proliferation of whatever is visible and the endless count of opinions polled and votes simulated. Appearance in general is thereby opposed by a homogeneous regime of the visible, and the democratic appearance of the people is strictly opposed by its simulated reality. But simulated reality is in no way the simulacrum's power to destroy the "real world" and its political avatars. Simulated reality is much more the final turning on its head of the truth proper to metapolitics. It is the organization of a specular relationship of opinion with itself, identical to the effectiveness of the sovereign people and to scientific knowledge of the behaviors of a population reduced to its statistical sample. Such a people, present in the form of its statistical reduction, is a people transformed into an object of knowledge and prediction that sends appearance and its polemics packing. From that moment exhaustive counting procedures can be introduced. The people is identical to the sum of its parts. The summation of its opinions is equal to the sum of the parts that constitute it. Their count is always even and with nothing left over. And this people absolutely equal to itself can also always be broken down into its reality: its socioprofessional categories and its age brackets. After that nothing can happen in the name of the people except a detailed elaboration of the opinions and interests of its exactly countable parts.

So the conjunction of science and the media is not the advent of egalitarian contingency. It is, in fact, exactly the opposite. It is the trapping of the equality of anyone and everyone in a series of equivalences and circularities that constitute the most radical form of forgetting all about it. The equality of anyone and everyone becomes the immediate effectiveness of a sovereign people, itself identical to scientific modeling and forecasting operating on an empirical population carved up exactly into its parts. The equality of anyone and everyone becomes identical to the total distribution of the people into its parts and subparts. The effectiveness of the sovereign people is exercised as strictly identical to the calculations of a science of the population's opinions, which is the same as saying an immediate unity of science and opinion. The "science of opinion" is indeed not merely a science taking "opinion" as its object. It is a science immediately accomplished as opinion, a science that has no meaning except in terms of this process of specularization where an opinion sees itself in the mirror held up by science to reveal to it its identity with itself. The unity with nothing left over of the sovereign people, of the empirical population and of the scientifically known population, is also the identity of opinion with its old

Platonic enemy, science. The reign of "simulation" is thus not the ruin of Platonic metaphysics and archipolitics. It is the paradoxical realization of their program: that community governed by science that puts everyone in their place, with the right opinion to match. The science of simulations of opinion is the perfect realization of the empty virtue Plato called *sôphrosunê:* the fact of each person's being in their place, going about their own business there, and having the opinion identical to the fact of being in that place and doing only what there is to do there. This virtue of identity, for Plato, presupposed that the simulacra created by mirrors and puppeteers were banished from town. But in the mirror that the science of opinion holds up to opinion, it appears that *opinion* can become the very name for being in one's place, that specularity can become the system of interiority that feeds each citizen and each part of the community the true image of what they are. *Sôphrosunê* was that paradoxical virtue that achieved the law of interiority of the community in exteriority, in terms of the sheer distribution of bodies, times, and spaces. The scientific mirror of opinion gives *sôphrosunê* its interiority as the unending — and true — relationship of the community to itself. Through such specularization, the regime of the full, the regime of the interiority of the community, is identical to the regime of the empty, of the people's dispersal. This "everyone in their place" can then show itself as being strictly identical to the equality of anyone and everyone, achieved as the fact of not thinking anything, as part of the population, other than what this part of the population thinks when it expresses its share of opinion. Postdemocratic "opinion" is the identity between the people and the population lived as a regime of interiority of a community that is aware of itself as the identity between the science of the whole and each person's opinion. This elimination of the appearance of the people and of its difference from itself then finds corresponding processes for eliminating the dispute by putting any object of dispute that might revive the name of the people and the appearances of its division in the form of a problem. This is actually the great transformation that the people's dispute undergoes, with the disappearance of its appearance and of its miscount.

Any dispute, in this system, becomes the name of a problem. And any problem can be reduced to a simple lack — a simple holding up — of the means to solve it. Identifying and dealing with the lack must then be substituted for the manifestation of wrong: the objectification of problems that will have to involve state action, from the margin of choice included, the expertise called on, the parts of the social body implicated, and the partners who need to be set up for the problems to be discussed. The democratic interlocutor was an unprecedented character, established to expose the dispute and set up the parties to it. The partner of postdemocracy, however, is identified with the existing part of society that the formulation of a problem implies in its solution. This is supposed to lead to the formation of opinion in the sense of a solution that imposes itself as the most reasonable, that is, as absolutely the only one objectively possible.

And so the ideal of an appropriateness between the managerial state and the legitimate state is affirmed through the removal of the demos and of the forms of dispute associated with its name and its various figures. Once the "archaic" actors of social conflict have been sent packing, the obstacle standing in the way of this compatibility evaporates. In its desire to establish harmony between names and things, the consensus model quite naturally puts Cratylus's old definition of *blaberon* back in the place of honor: *blaberon* is what "turns off the current." The old figures of wrong and its subjectification block the free current of *sumpheron*, which, according to its etymology, "sweeps along together" merchandise and ideas, persons and groups. The dissolution of the archaic figures of conflict allows the exact progression from *sumpheron* to *dikaïon*, the free circulation of right in the social body, the growing appropriateness of the juridical norm to free economic and social initiative through extension of rights and their flexible adaptation to the endless movements of the economy and of society, lifestyles, and attitudes.

So consensus, before becoming the reasonable virtue of individuals and groups who agree to discuss their problems and build up their interests, is a determined regime of the perceptible, a particular mode of visibility of *right* as *arkhê* of the community. Before problems can be settled by well-behaved social partners, the rule of conduct of the dispute has to be settled, as a specific structure of community. The identity of the community with itself must be posited, along with the rule of right as identical to the elimination of wrong. There is a lot of talk about how the extension of the legitimate state and the sphere of law is characteristic of our regimes, but, beyond agreement that the rule is preferable to the arbitrary and liberty to servitude, it remains to be seen precisely what phenomena are indicated by this. Like every word at stake in politics, the word "law" is a homonym for quite different things: the juridical provisions of codes and ways of implementing them, philosophical notions of community and what it is based on, political structures of wrong, modes of police management of the relations between the state and social groups and interests. Simple celebration of the legitimate state then takes convenient shortcuts that allow us, in the face of the nonright of archipolice states, to bundle all these heterogeneous "rights" together in a single unquestioned rule of law, characterized by a happy harmony between the legislative activity of the public authorities, the rights of individuals, and the procedural inventiveness of law offices. But the rule of *the* law is always the rule of *a* law, that is, of a regime of unity among all the different senses of the law posited as a regime of identity of the community. Today, the identification between democracy and the legitimate state is used to produce a regime of the community's identity as itself, to make politics evaporate under a concept of law that identifies it with the spirit of the community.

This law/spirit of the community today reveals itself in movement between two poles of identity: at one end, it represents the stable essence of *dikaïon* through which the community is itself; at the other, this essence comes to be identified with the multiple play of *sumpheron*, which constitutes the dynamism of society. The spread of the legal sphere takes two main forms in Western systems, before and after the intervention of government power. Before government power, legislative action is submitted increasingly to a scholarly legal authority, to expert sages who say what is in keeping with the spirit of the constitution and the essence of the community it defines. Here one gladly salutes a recasting of democracy along the founding lines of liberalism, the submission of politics, in the person of the state, to the juridical rule embodying the social contract that places individual liberties and social energies in community. But this alleged submission of the state-based to the juridical sphere is actually submission of the political to the state-based via the juridical, the exercise of a capacity to strip politics of its initiative through which the state precedes and legitimizes itself. This is indeed the curious mode of legitimization covered by the theories of "small" government in vogue. The modern state, they say, means small government, a government that gives back to the legal sphere, on the one hand, the social sphere, on the other, all it once took from them. But it is not so much in relation to itself as in relation to politics that the state practices such modesty. What it tends to make disappear by becoming so modest is certainly less its own apparatus than the political stage for exposing and processing conflict, the community stage that brought the separate worlds together. Thus the practice of the "constitutionality checkup" is not so much the submission of the legislative and the executive to the "government of the Bench" as a declaration of "no case to answer" for any public manifestation of conflict. This is really state mimesis of the political practice of litigation. Such a mimesis transforms the traditional argument that gives place to the show of democracy, the internal gap in equality, into a problem that is a matter for expert knowledge.

It is this mimesis that, in fact, orders the ritual theater of referral of a case to the court of the supreme constitutional body. The knowledge required of the high-court judge actually has absolutely nothing to do with the science of constitutional texts and their interpretation. It is sheer enunciation of the identity of equality with itself in its difference. The legal art of whoever refers a case to the constitutional judges always comes down to presenting the law or the undesirable article of law as contradictory not to some article or other of the constitution but to the very spirit of the constitution, indeed to the principle of equality as expressed in the first article of the Declaration of the Rights of Man. The "juridical" argument of unconstitutionality thus constructs a parody of the democratic dispute that put the egalitarian text to the test with cases of inequality. The argument of the dispute, the setting up of the divided community, is caricatured in these reasons adduced, which are able to detect a contradiction with the principle of equality, the soul of the constitution, in any old insignificant article of any undesirable law. The constitutional judge can then respond to this transformation of the political dispute into a legal problem with a lesson in law that is nothing more than the first axiom of "political philosophy," that concerning the difference in equalities, which, ever since Plato, has gone like this: the principle of equality is to give similar things to similar beings and dissimilar things to dissimilar beings. Equality, say the constitutional judges in their wisdom, must apply in all circumstances (Declaration of the Rights of Man, article 1), but under different conditions authorized by the difference in circumstances (article 6). The law is thereby in accordance with the balance of the two equalities, except for the articles that are not in accordance.

Such wisdom, which divests politics of its job, has a twofold benefit. First, it places any obscure quarrel (the composition of university boards or the retirement age for professors at the Collège de France) in the element of ideality of the relationship of the Declaration of the Rights of Man with itself. The "juridical" demonstration of the soul of the community's identity with itself then completes the scientific/mediatic demonstration of opinion's identity with itself. But it also endows state power with a most specific form of legitimacy. The "modest" state is a state that evacuates politics, that relinquishes, in a word, what does not belong to it — the dispute of the people — in order to increase its property, to further develop its own legitimization processes. The state today legitimizes itself by declaring that politics is impossible. And this demonstration of impossibility works through a demonstration of its own impotence. To evacuate the demos, postdemocracy has to evacuate politics, using the pincers of economic necessity and juridical rule, even if it means bringing both of these together in the definition of a new citizenry in which the power and powerlessness of each and every one has come to even out.

This is what that other form now caught up in the extension of the juridical shows, somewhat on the other side of government action. We are effectively witnessing an active multiplying and redefining of rights, aimed at getting law, rights, the rule of law, and the legal ideal circulating throughout society, at adapting to and anticipating all the movements of society. So family law seeks to emulate and if possible anticipate any new attitudes and moral values and the looser ties these define, all the while involving the participants in the resolution of their problems. Property law is ceaselessly running to catch up with the intangible property linked to the new technologies. Committees of savants, gathered together in the name of bioethics, promise to clarify for the legislator the point at which man's humanity begins. In the meantime, members of the legislature vote in support of laws to limit the corruption presiding over the financing of their parties and to prohibit historians from falsifying history. As for the right to work, it, like work itself, has tended to become "flexible." It seeks to adapt to all the movements of the economy and to all the shifts in the employment market, embracing the mobile identity of a worker constantly liable to become a half-worker, downright unemployed, or semi-unemployed. This adaptation is not only the grim realism that observes that for workers to have rights, they must first work, and that for them to work they must agree to whittle away the rights that prevent enterprises from giving them work; it is also the transformation of the law into the idea of the law and of parties, beneficiaries of the law fighting for their rights, into individuals who hold a right identical to the exercise of their responsibility as citizens. The right of the worker thus becomes the citizenship of the worker, once they have become a party to the collective enterprise at the same time as the enterprise that employs them. And this citizenship is as liable to get involved in an adult education accord or an assimilation contract as in the traditional and conflict-ridden framework of the employment contract. The old "rigidities" of law and the struggle for "rights" are opposed by the flexibility of a right mirroring social flexibility, of a citizenship that makes each individual a microcosm in which is reflected the identity with itself of the community of energies and responsibilities that look like rights.

So all these extensions of law and of the legitimate state are first the constitution of a figure of law whereby the idea behind it is occasionally developed to the detriment of the forms of its existence. They are also extensions of the ability of the expert state to evacuate politics by eliminating any interval between law and fact. On the one hand, the law now divests the state of the politics of which it once divested the people; on the other, it now latches on to every situation, every possible dispute, breaking it down into its components as a problem and transforming the parties to the dispute into social performers, reflecting the community's identity with itself as the law of their acting. The growing identification of the real and the rational, law and expertise, right and a system of guarantees that are primarily guarantees of state power, the ever-intensified assurance of its infallibility, of the impossibility of its being unjust, except by mistake, a mistake that it never ceases to guard itself against by endlessly consulting experts on the twofold legitimacy of what it is doing — all these are extensions of this process.

A conjunction of three phenomena then occurs: the spread of law, the practice of generalized expertise, and practice of the eternal opinion poll. Law and fact become as indistinguishable as reality and its image, as the real and the possible. The expert state eliminates every interval of appearance, of subjectification, and of dispute in an exact concordance between the order of law and the order of the facts. What the state relinquishes by having itself incessantly checked, what it continually acknowledges in individuals and groups in ever new rights, it regains in legitimization. The power of law is more and more identified with this spiraling overlegitimization of the educated state: in the growing equivalence of the production of relationships of law and management of market forces, in endless cross-referencing of law and reality whose final word is pure and simple identification of democratic "form" with the managerial practice of bowing to commercial necessity. At the end of the day, proof of the right of state power is identical to the evidence that it only ever does the only thing possible, only ever what is required by strict necessity in the context of the growing intricacy of economies within the global market.

The legitimacy of state power is thereby reinforced by the very affirmation of its impotence, of its lack of choice faced with the worldwide necessity it is dominated by. The theme of the common will is replaced by that of the lack of personal will, of capacity for autonomous action that is anything more than just management of necessity. From an allegedly defunct Marxism, the supposedly reigning liberalism borrows the theme of objective necessity, identified with the constraints and caprices of the world market. Marx's once-scandalous thesis that governments are simple business agents for international capital is today obvious fact on which "liberals" and "socialists" agree. The absolute identification of politics with the management of capital is no longer the shameful secret hidden behind the "forms" of democracy; it is the openly declared truth by which our governments acquire legitimacy. In this process of legitimization, any demonstration of capability needs to be based on a demonstration of powerlessness. The dreams of politically astute housewives at the stove or of simple laborers rising up against fate are opposed by the theme of a reverse Marxism: optimizing the pleasures of individuals is only possible on the basis of their acknowledged inability to manage the conditions of this optimization. The state then establishes its authority based on its ability to internalize common powerlessness, to determine the thin ground, the "almost nothing" of a possible on which everyone's prosperity as well as the maintenance of the community bond depends. On the one hand, this almost nothing is posited as so little it is not worth the trouble of fighting over with the managers of the state machine. But, on the other hand, it is posited as the decisive minute difference that separates the prosperity to come from the misery hanging over us, the social bond from looming chaos, a minute difference too decisive and too sustained not to be left to the experts, to those who know how, by placing 0.5 percent of the Gross National Product on one side rather than on the other, we pass over to the good or the bad side of the line, from prosperity to the brink of ruin, from social peace to a general coming apart at the seams. Management of abundance thus becomes identical with crisis management. It is management of the sole possible necessity that must be incessantly anticipated, followed, planned, put off, day in, day out. The management of this "almost nothing" is also an uninterrupted demonstration of the identity between the legitimate state and the expert state, of the identity between the power of this state and its powerlessness, a power that internalizes the identity of the great power of enterprising and contracting individuals and groups with the powerlessness of the demos as a political force.

This exact sameness is missed by both pessimistic and optimistic analysts of postindustrial society. The pessimists decry the social disintegration brought about by the collapse of collective constraints and legitimizations as a result of rampant democratic individualism and hedonism. The optimists, on the contrary, crow about the growing correlation between the free flaunting of merchandise, free democratic suffrage, and the aspirations of narcissistic individualism. Both thus agree in describing a state of emptiness, the emptiness of community legitimizations, even though this may be interpreted either as a Hobbesian black hole of the war of all against all, or as the final demolition of the archipolitics of the community. Both camps thus overlook the equivalence between the empty and the full that characterizes postdemocratic metapolitics. The declared state of emptiness or disintegration is just as much a state of saturation of the community by the detailed counting of its parts and the specular relationship whereby each part engages with the whole. To those who deplore the loss of republican citizenship, postdemocratic logic responds by proclaiming generalized citizenship. And so the town is called on to embody the identity of urban civilization with the community of the polis animated by its community soul. The citizen-enterprise is called on to show the identity of their productive and appropriating energy with the part played in the building of the community and the putting together of a microcosm of this community. Through the citizenry of the local area and that of the association, this requirement reaches the individual, called on to be the microcosm of the great noisy whole of the circulation and un-interrupted exchange of rights and capabilities, goods and the Good. In the mirror of Narcissus, it is the essence of such a community that is reflected. The "individual" sees himself in it, is required to see himself in it as his own militant, as a small alliance-forming energy, running from one tie to the next, from one contract to the next as well as from one thrill to the next. What is reflected through this individual is the identity of the community with itself, the identity of the networks of society's energy and of the circuits of state legitimization.

So if we assume that the logic of consensus leads us toward the same old black hole of the war of all against all, it is for very different reasons than those cited by the "pessimists." The problem is not simply that "democratic individualism" determines each individual's expectation of a satisfaction their state cannot guarantee. It is more especially that in proclaiming the effectiveness of the identity between the legitimate state and the rights of individuals, in making each person the reflection of the soul of the community of energies and rights, consensual logic sets everywhere the boundary between peace and war, the breaking point at which the community is exposed to a demonstration of its untruth. In other words, "disintegration" is another name for this saturation that knows no other form of being-in-common than the specular link between individual satisfaction and the state's auto-demonstration. It is a negative demonstration of the fanaticism of the tie that binds individuals and groups together in a fabric with no holes, no gap between names and things, rights and facts, individuals and subjects, with no intervals in which forms of community in dispute, nonspecular forms of community, may be constructed. This helps to make sense of why the theory of the social contract and the idea of a "new citizenry" have today found a privileged conceptual terrain: that of the medicine applied to what is known as "exclusion." This is because the "fight against exclusion" is also the paradoxical conceptual place where exclusion emerges as just another name for consensus.

Consensus thinking conveniently represents what it calls "exclusion" in the simple relationship between an inside and an outside. But what is at stake under the name of exclusion is not being-outside. It is the mode of division according to which an inside and an outside can be joined. The "exclusion" talked about today is a most determined form of such a partition. It is the very invisibility of the partition, the effacing of any marks that might allow the relationship between community and noncommunity to be argued about within some political mechanism of subjectification. In the days when police logic could express itself without having to be tarted up, it said, with Bonald, that "certain persons are in society without being of society" or, with Guizot, that politics is the business of "men of leisure." A dividing line separated the private world of noise, of darkness and inequality, on the one side, from the public world of the logos, of equality and shared meaning, on the other. Exclusion could thus be symbolized, polemically constructed, as a relationship between two worlds and the demonstration of their litigious community. The uncounted could make themselves count by showing up the process of division and breaking in on others' equality and appropriating it for themselves. The "exclusion" referred to today is, on the contrary, the very absence of a representable barrier. And so it is strictly identical to the law of consensus.

What indeed is consensus if not the presupposition of inclusion of all parties and their problems that prohibits the political subjectification of a part of those who have no part, of a count of the uncounted? Everyone is included in advance, every individual is the nucleus and image of a community of opinions that are equal to parties, of problems that are reducible to shortages, and of rights that are identical to energies. In this "classless" society, the barrier has been replaced by a continuum of positions, starting at the top and going all the way to the bottom, mimicking basic school grading. Exclusion is no longer subjectified in this continuum, is no longer included in it. Beyond an invisible, unsubjectifiable line, you are simply out of the picture and from then on you are countable only in the aggregate of those present: the aggregate of those who not only lack work, resources, and housing, but also lack "identity" and "social ties," who are not able to be those inventive alliance-forming individuals made to internalize and reflect the great collective achievement. In aid of such people, the powers that be then make an effort at additional saturation, designed to stop the gaps that, in separating them from themselves, separate them from the community. The powers that be go out of their way to provide those little extras of missing identity and ties in lieu of jobs, which the authorities simply do not have. A personal medicine aimed at restoring *identities* then joins forces with a societal medicine aimed at mending the community fabric, to give back to each person excluded the identity of a mobilized capability and responsibility, to establish in every derelict dwelling a cell of collective responsibility. The social reject and the abandoned urban wasteland then become models of a "new social contract" and a new citizenry, thrown up at the very point where the responsibility of the individual and the cement of the social bond were crumbling. Some extraordinary minds and souls are employed in this process, and the results are not negligible. There remains the circularity of a logic aimed at sticking the supplement of a bond everywhere in society as well as motivation in the individual, when the problem with either sphere is strictly the effect of such an unstoppable saturation endeavor and of the unconditional requirement of mobilization. There remains as well the demonstration of the exact identity between sickness and health, the norm of saturation of consensus and the dereliction of downtrodden identities. The war of all against all, the constitution of each individual as a threat to the community, are the strict correlate of the consensual requirement of a community wholly realized as the identity between the people and the population reflected in each person. Eliminating wrong, as consensus society demands, is identical to absolutizing it.

This equivalence is illustrated by the violent intrusion of new forms of racism and xenophobia into our consensus regimes. It is no doubt possible to come up with all kinds of economic and sociological reasons for this: unemployment (causing people to accuse the foreigner of taking the local's place), unbridled urbanization, the dereliction of the suburbs and dormitory towns. But all these "socioeconomic" causes that are attributed to a political phenomenon in fact designate entities inscribed in the political issue of the partition of the perceptible. The factory and its disappearance, work as employment and work as a structure of being-in-common, unemployment as lack of work and unemployment as "an identity problem," the distribution and redistribution of workers in spaces defined by their distance from the workplace and those spaces where the common is visible — all these concern the relationship between the police configuration of the perceptible and the possibilities of setting up within it the visibility of litigious objects and disputing subjects. The nature of the combination of all these elements belongs to a mode of visibility that either neutralizes or points the finger at the otherness of the foreigner. It is from this standpoint that we can discuss the simple inference of the undesirability of immigrants from their too-high number. Clearly, the cutoff point of undesirability is not a matter of statistics. We had nearly the same number of immigrants twenty years ago. But they had another name then: they were called migrant workers or just plain workers. Today's immigrant is first a worker who has lost his second name, who has lost the political form of his identity and of his otherness, the form of a political subjectification of the count of the uncounted. All he now has left is a sociological identity, which then topples over into the anthropological nakedness of a different race and skin. What he has lost is his identification with a mode of subjectification of the people, worker or proletarian, as object of a declared wrong *and* as subject giving form to his dispute. It is the loss of the *one-more* of subjectification that determines the constitution of a *one-too-many* as phobia of the community.

The end of the "myths" of class struggle has been loudly trumpeted, and some have even gone as far as to identify the disappearance of factories, now wiped off the urban landscape, with the demolition of myths and utopias. But perhaps now they are beginning to see how naive such "antiutopianism" is. What is known as the end of "myths" is the end of forms of visibility of the collective space, the end of the visibility of the gap between politics and sociology, between subjectification and identity. The end of the "myths" of the people, the invisibility of workers, is the "case dismissed" of modes of subjectification that allowed a person to be included as excluded, to be counted as uncounted.

The wiping out of these political modes of appearance and subjectification of the dispute results in the abrupt reappearance in the real of an otherness that can no longer be symbolized. The erstwhile worker is thus split in two: on the one hand, the immigrant; on the other, this new racist on whom sociologists significantly pin another color label, "white trash," *petits blancs*, the name once attributed to the humble settlers of French Algeria. The separation that was excluded from visibility as archaic reappears in the even more archaic form of naked otherness. Well-meaning consensus in vain offers its roundtables to discuss the problem of immigrants. Here as elsewhere the cure and the disease form a vicious circle. Postdemocratic objectification of the immigration "problem" goes hand in hand with fixation on a radical otherness, an object of absolute, prepolitical hate. In the same movement the figure of the other is exaggerated in pure racist rejection and evaporates in the problematization of immigration. The new visibility of the other in all the nakedness of their intolerable difference is strictly a hangover from the consensus operation. It is the "reasonable" and "peaceful" effacing of appearance in the total exhibition of the real, of the miscount of the people in the breakdown of the population, and of the dispute in the consensus that pulls the monster of radical otherness back into line with the failing of politics. It is the exhaustive breakdown of the interminably polled population that produces, in place of the people declared archaic, this subject called "the French," who turn up, alongside prognostics about the "political" future of this or that undersecretary of state, in a few decidedly uncompromising opinions about the excessive number of foreigners and the inadequacy of the crackdown on them. These opinions are, of course, at the same time demonstrations of the very nature of opinions in a media regime, the way they are at once real and simulated. The subject of the opinion says what he thinks of Blacks and Arabs in the same real/simulated mode in which he is elsewhere invited to tell all about his fantasies and to

119

completely satisfy these just by dialing four figures and as many letters. The subject who opines accordingly is the subject of this new mode of the visible where everything is on display, up for grabs, a subject called on to live out all his fantasies in a world of total exhibition and of the asymptotic coming together of bodies, in this "everything is possible" of thrills displayed and promised — meaning, of course, doomed to disappointment: the subject being urged accordingly to search and destroy the "bad body," the diabolical body that everywhere stands in the way of the total satisfaction everywhere within reach and everywhere snatched from one's grasp.

The new racism of advanced societies thus owes its singularity to being the point of intersection for all forms of the community's identity with itself that go to define the consensus model — as well as all forms of defection from this identity and of compensation for such defection. So it is only normal that the law should now round off this coherence, in other words, turn its unity into the mode of reflection of a community separating itself from its Other. In dealing with the problem of immigrants, the law, of course, proposes to act for justice and peace. By defining rules of assimilation and exclusion until now left to the luck of the draw and to disparities in the regulations, it claims to be bringing the particular into the sphere of its universality. By separating good foreigners from undesirables, it is meant to be disarming racism, which feeds off lumping everyone together. The problem is that this distinction itself can only be made at the cost of putting a face to this indefinable Other who excites feelings of fear and rejection. The law, which is supposed to sort out the confusion of "feeling," does so only at the cost of borrowing its object, its way of uniting, without any underlying concept, heterogeneous cases of the other's unacceptability, and of handing it back subsumed in a conceptual unity. The law decreed by the consensus system is also confirmation of the kind of relationship with oneself that the consensus system itself constitutes. Its principle is to establish continual convertibility from the *one* of the law to the *one* of feeling that defines being-together. The work of consensual law is thus first to devise the schema that transforms the felt but indefinable *one* of rejection into *one* of common law. It is this schema that constitutes the untraceable object "immigrant" by unifying the heterogeneous cases of the juvenile delinquent of North African origin, the Sri Lankan worker without papers, the polygamous Muslim, and the worker from Mali who forces the upkeep of his family on the French community. The circulation of a few converters, such as "clandestine," which joins the figure of the foreigner to that of the delinquent, boosts the schema, providing an object for the law similar to the object of feeling: the figure of the overabundant multiple that reproduces itself lawlessly. The schema of consensual law thus ties together the order of *nomos* as the power to agree and to enter into contracts with the order of *phusis* as the power to con-sent. Consensus is a circular relationship between nature and the law that leaves to the latter the problem of determining the antinature experienced by the former as intolerable. The law does this by separating *phusis,* conceived as the power of whatever flourishes, from this antinature, conceived as the power of the proliferating multiple. The law achieves nature by identifying what nature once spontaneously indicated as its disease, this multitude that never stops reproducing itself. Lawyers of remotest ancient Rome made up a name for such a multitude: *proletarii,* those who do nothing but reproduce their own multiplicity and who, for this very reason, do not deserve to be counted. Modern democracy disinterred the word and made it a political subject: an odd multiple by which the uncounted are counted, an operative distancing productive and reproductive bodies from themselves, an analyzer dividing the community from itself. Metapolitics transformed it into the ambiguous figure of the ultrapolitical subject of the true movement dissipating the political illusion. As a nihilistic polishing off of metapolitics, consensual postdemocracy eradicates the term, buckling the community back on itself and sending the figure back to its very beginnings: short of democracy, short of politics.

Chapter 6

Politics in Its Nihilistic Age

To recapitulate: politics exists wherever the count of parts and parties of society is disturbed by the inscription of a part of those who have no part. It begins when the equality of anyone and everyone is inscribed in the liberty of the people. This liberty of the people is an empty property, an improper property through which those who are nothing purport that their group is identical to the whole of the community. Politics exists as long as singular forms of subjectification repeat the forms of the original inscription of the identity between the whole of the community and the nothing that separates it from itself—in other words, the sole count of its parts. Politics ceases wherever this gap no longer has any place, wherever the whole of the community is reduced to the sum of its parts with nothing left over.

There are several ways of thinking of the whole as the sole sum of its parts. The sum may be made up of individuals, small machines intensely exploiting their own freedom to desire, to undertake, and to enjoy. It may be made up of social groups building their interests as responsible partners. It may be made up of communities, each endowed with recognition of its identity and its culture. In this regard, the consensual state is tolerant. But what it no longer tolerates is the supernumerary party, the one that throws out the count of the community. What it needs is real parties, having both their own properties and the common property of the whole. What it cannot tolerate is a nothing that is all. The consensus system rests on these solid axioms: the whole is all, nothing is nothing. By eliminating the parasitical entities of political subjectification, little by little the identity of the whole with the all is obtained, which is the identity of the principle of the whole with that of each of its parts, beneficiaries of the whole. This identity is called humanity.

And this is where the trouble starts. The consensus system celebrated its victory over totalitarianism as the final victory of law over nonlaw and of realism over utopias. It was gearing up to welcome into its space—freed from politics and called Europe—the democracies born of the destruction of the totalitarian states. But just about everywhere it looks it sees the landscape of humanity, freed from totalitarianism and the utopias, as a landscape of fundamentalisms of identity. On the ruins of the totalitarian states, ethnicism and ethnic wars break out. Religion and religious states once consecrated as a natural barrier to Soviet expansion take on the figure of the fundamentalist threat. This threat even springs up in the heart of consensus states, wherever those workers who are no longer anything more than immigrants live, wherever individuals turn out to be incapable of meeting the requirement that they militate for their own integrity. In the face of this threat, consensus communities witness the rebirth of sheer rejection of those whose ethnicity or religion cannot be borne. The consensus system represents itself to itself as the world of law as opposed to the world of nonlaw— the world of barbaric identity, religion, or ethnicity. But in that world of subjects strictly identified with their ethnicity, their race, or with that people guided by divine light, in these wars between tribes fighting to occupy the entire territory of those who share their identity, the consensus system also contemplates the extreme caricature of its reasonable dream: a world cleansed of surplus identities, peopled by real bodies endowed with properties expressed by their name. The consensus system announced a world beyond the demos, a world made up of individuals and groups simply showing common humanity. It over-looked just one thing: between individuals and humanity, there is always a partition of the perceptible, a configuration that determines the way in which the different parties have a part in the community. And there are two main modes of division: counting a part of those who have no part and not counting such a part—the demos or the ethnos. The consensus system thought its expansion was boundless: Europe, the international community, the citizenry of the world, and, finally, humanity—all so many names for a whole that is equal to the sum of its elements, each having the common property of the whole. What it discovers is a new, radical figure of the identity between all and nothing. The new figure, the nonpolitical figure of the all identical to nothing, of an *integrity* everywhere under attack, is also, from now on, called *humanity*. Man "born free and everywhere in chains" has become man born human and everywhere inhuman.

Beyond the forms of democratic dispute, what is indeed spreading is the reign of a humanity equal to itself, directly attributed to each one, exposed in each one to its own shattering; an all inhabited by its nothingness, a humanity showing itself, demonstrating itself everywhere to be denied. The end of the great subjectifications of wrong is not the end of the age of the "universal victim"; it is, on the contrary, its beginning. The militant democracy of old went through a whole series of polemical forms of "men born free and equal in law." The various forms of "us" have taken on different subject names to try the litigious power of "human rights," to put the inscription of equality to the test, to ask if human rights, the rights of man, were more or less than the rights of the citizen, if they were those of woman, of the proletarian, of the black man and the black woman, and so on. And so "we" have given human rights all the power they could possibly have: the power of the inscription of equality amplified by the power of its rationale and its expression in the construction of litigious cases, in the linking of a world where the inscription of equality is valid and the world where it is not valid. The reign of the "humanitarian" begins, on the other hand, wherever human rights are cut off from any capacity for polemical particularization of their universality, where the egalitarian phrase ceases to be phrased, interpreted in the arguing of a wrong that manifests its litigious effectiveness. Humanity is then no longer polemically attributed to women or to proles, to blacks or to the damned of the earth. Human rights are no longer experienced as political capacities. The predicate "human" and "human rights" are simply attributed, without any phrasing, without any mediation, to their eligible party, the subject "man." The age of the "humanitarian" is one of immediate identity between the ordinary example of suffering humanity and the plenitude of the subject of humanity and of its rights. The eligible party pure and simple is then none other than the wordless victim, the ultimate figure of the one excluded from the logos, armed only with a voice expressing a monotonous moan, the moan of naked suffering, which saturation has made inaudible. More precisely, this person who is merely human then boils down to the couple of the victim, the pathetic figure of a person to whom such humanity is denied, and the executioner, the monstrous figure of a person who denies humanity. The "humanitarian" regime of the "international community" then exercises the administration of human rights in their regard, by sending supplies and medicine to the one and airborne divisions, more rarely, to the other.[1]

The transformation of the democratic stage into a humanitarian stage may be illustrated by the impossibility of any mode of enunciation. At the beginning of the May '68 movement in France, the demonstrators defined a form of subjectification summed up in a single phrase: "We are all German Jews." This phrase is a good example of the heterological mode of political subjectification: the stigmatizing phrase of the enemy, keen to track down the intruder on the stage where the classes and *their* parties were counted, was taken at face value, then twisted around and turned into the open subjectification of the uncounted, a name that could not possibly be confused with any real social group, with anyone's actual particulars.

Obviously, a phrase of this kind would be unspeakable today for two reasons. The first is that it is not accurate: those who spoke it were not German and the majority of them were not Jewish. Since that time, the advocates of progress as well as those of law and order have decided to accept as legitimate only those claims made by real groups that take the floor in person and themselves state their own identity. No one has the right now to call themselves a prole, a black, a Jew, or a woman if they are not, if they do not possess native entitlement and the social experience. "Humanity" is, of course, the exception to this rule of authenticity; humanity's authenticity is to be speechless, its rights are back in the hands of the international community police. And this is where the second reason the phrase is now unspeakable comes in: because it is obviously indecent. Today the identity "German Jew" immediately signifies the identity of the victim of the crime against humanity that no one can claim without profanation. It is no longer a name available for political subjectification but the name of the absolute victim that suspends such subjectification. The subject of contention has become the name of what is out of bounds. The age of humanitarianism is an age where the notion of the absolute victim debars polemical games of subjectification of wrong. The episode known as the "new philosophy" is entirely summed up in this prescription: the notion of massacre stops thought in its tracks as unworthy and prohibits politics. The notion of the irredeemable then splits consensual realism: political dispute is impossible for two reasons, because its violence cripples reasonable agreement between parties and because the facetiousness of its polemical embodiments is an insult to the victims of absolute wrong. Politics must then yield before massacre, thought bow out before the unthinkable.

Only, the doubling of the consensual logic of submission to the sole count of parties with the ethical/humanitarian logic of submission to the unthinkable of genocide starts to look like a *double bind*. The distribution of roles, it is true, may allow the two logics to be exercised separately, but only unless some provocateur comes along and lashes out at their point of intersection, a point they so obviously point to, all the while pretending not to see it. This point is the possibility of the crime against humanity's being thinkable as the entirety of extermination. This is the point where the negationist provocation strikes, turning the logic of the administrators of the possible and the thinkers

127

of the unthinkable back on them, by wielding the twin argument of the impossibility of an exhaustive count of extermination and of its unthinkability as an idea, by asserting the impossibility of presenting the victim of the crime against humanity and of providing a sufficient reason why the executioner would have perpetrated it.

This is in effect the double thrust of the negationist argument to deny the reality of the extermination of the Jews in the Nazi camps. It plays on the classic sophist paradoxes of the unending count and division ad infinitum. As early as 1950, Paul Rassinier fixed the parameters of negationism's sales pitch in the form of a series of questions whose answers let it appear every time that, even if all the elements of the process were established, their connections could never be entirely proved and still less could it be proved that they were a result of a plan entirely worked out, programmed and immanent in each of its steps.[2] Most certainly, said Rassinier, there were Nazi proclamations advocating the extermination of all Jews. But declarations have never in themselves killed anyone. Most certainly, there were plans for gas chambers. But a plan for a gas chamber and a working gas chamber are two different things — as different as a hundred potential talers and a hundred real talers. Most certainly, there were gas chambers actually installed in a certain number of camps. But a gas chamber is only ever a gasworks that one can use for all sorts of things, and nothing about it proves that it has the specific function of mass extermination. Most certainly, there were, in all the camps, regular selections at the end of which prisoners disappeared and were never seen again. But there are thousands of ways of killing people or simply letting them die, and those who disappeared will never be able to tell us how they disappeared. Most certainly, finally, there were prisoners in the camps who were effectively gassed. But there is nothing to prove that they were the victims of a systematic overall plan and not of simple sadistic torturers.

We should pause for a moment to look at the two prongs of this line of argument: Rassinier claimed in 1950 that the documents that would establish a logical connection between all these facts, linking them as one unique event, were missing. He also added that it was doubtful they would ever be found. Since then, though, documents have been found in sufficient abundance, but the revisionist provocation still has not given in. On the contrary, it has found new followers, a new level of acceptance. The more its arguments have revealed themselves to be inconsistent on the factual level, the more its real force has been shored up. This force is to damage the very system of belief according to which a series of facts is established as a singular event and as an event subsumed in the category of the possible. It is to damage the point where two possibilities must be adjusted to each other: the material possibility of the crime as a total linking of its sequences and its intellectual possibility according to its qualification as absolute crime against humanity. The negationist provocation stands up not because of the proofs it uses to oppose the accumulation of adverse proofs. It stands up because it leads each of the logics confronting each other in it to a critical point where impossibility finds itself established in one or another of its figures: as a missing link in the chain or the impossibility of thinking the link. It then forces these logics into a series of conflicting movements whereby the possible is always caught up by the impossible and verification of the event by the thought of what is unthinkable in it.

The first aporia is that of the law and of the judge. French public opinion cried out against the judges who let ex-militiaman Paul Touvier off on the charge of the "crime against humanity." But before we get indignant, we should reflect on the peculiar configuration of the relationships between the law, politics, and science implied in such a matter. The juridical notion of the "crime against humanity," initially annexed to war crimes, was freed from those to allow the pursuit of crimes that legal prescriptions and government amnesties had allowed to go unpunished. The sorry fact is that nothing by rights defines the *humanity* that is the object of the crime. The crime is then established not because it is recognized that humanity has been attacked in its victim, but because it is recognized that the agent who carried it out was, at the time of its execution, an underling simply obeying the collective planned will of a state "practicing a policy of ideological hegemony." The judge is then required to become a historian in order to establish the

existence of such a policy, to trace the continuity from the original intention of a state to the action of one of its servants, at the risk of once
again ending up in the aporias of division ad infinitum. The original
judges of militiaman Touvier did not find the continuous thread of a
"policy of ideological hegemony" leading from the birth of the Vichy
State to the criminal act of that state's militiaman. The second lot of
judges resolved the problem by making Touvier a direct subordinate
of the German Nazi State. The accused argued in his defense that he
showed humanity by doing *less* than the planned collective will required
him to do. Let us suppose for a moment that an accused were to put
forward conversely that he did *more*, that he acted without orders and
without ideological motivation, out of pure personal sadism. Such an
accused would be no more than an ordinary monster, escaping the legal
framework of the crime against humanity, clearly revealing the impossibility of the judge's putting together the agent and the patient of the
crime against humanity.

The aporia of the judge and of the law then becomes that of the science required in the matter, that is, the science of history. As specialists, historians have wheeled in all the proofs demanded to establish
the facts and the way they are linked. As a scientific body, they have
protested against the negationists' pseudoscientific methods. We might
then wonder why various states need to endow themselves with laws
banning the falsification of history through denial of the extermination.
The answer is simple: the history that can call in all the countertesti-
mony proper to refuting a party in a normal court reveals itself to be
simply incapable of responding to two arguments, the argument that a
succession of facts all linked to each other never reaches the point where
it constitutes a unique event and the argument that an event does not
take place in time unless that time makes its possibility possible. It is incapable of responding because these arguments are of a piece with the
system of belief according to which history thinks of itself as a science:
the system that submits the thinkableness of a thought's effectiveness
to the possibility that its time makes it possible.

This is the double catch on which the negationist argument plays. The impossibility of establishing the event of the extermination in its totality is supported by the impossibility of thinking the extermination as belonging to the reality of its time. The paradoxes that distinguish formal cause from material cause and efficient cause from final cause would have rapidly run out of steam if they merely reflected the impossibility of the four causes being able to be joined into one single sufficient principle of reason. Beyond the quibbling about the composition of the gases and the means of producing sufficient quantity, the negationist provocation calls on the "reason" of the historian in order to ask if, in their capacity as an educated person, they can find in the modes of rationality (which complex industrial and state systems in our century obey) the necessary and sufficient reason for a great modern state's abandoning itself to the designation and mass extermination of a radical enemy. The historian, who has all the facts at their fingertips ready to respond, then is caught in the trap of the notion that governs historical reasoning: for a fact to be admitted, it must be thinkable; for it to be thinkable, it must belong to what its time makes thinkable for its imputation not to be anachronistic. In a famous book, Lucien Febvre alleges that Rabelais was not a nonbeliever.[3] Not that we have any proof that he was not — that kind of truth is precisely a matter for the judge, not the historian. The truth of the historian is that Rabelais was not a nonbeliever because it was not possible for him to be, because his time did not offer the possibility of this possibility. The thought event consisting in the clear and simple position of not believing was impossible according to this particular truth: the truth of what a period in time makes thinkable, of what it authorizes the existence. To break out of this truth is to commit a mortal sin as far as the science of history goes: the sin of anachronism.

How does one get from that impossibility to the impossibility that the extermination took place? Not only through the perversity of the provocateur who carries a certain reasoning to the point of absurdity and scandal, but also through the overturning of the metapolitical regime of truth. Lucien Febvre's truth was that of a sociological organicism, of the representation of society as a body governed by the homogeneity of collective attitudes and common beliefs. This solid truth has become a hollow truth. The necessary subscription of all individual thought to the common belief system of one's time has become just the hollowness of a negative ontological argument: what is not possible according to one's time is impossible. What is impossible cannot have been. The formal play of the negative ontological argument thereby chimes with the "reasonable" opinion that a great modern industrial state like Germany had no need to invent the insanity of the extermination of the Jews. The historian who has refuted all the liar's proofs cannot radically refute his lie because he cannot refute the idea of the truth that sustains it. The historian brings to the judge the connection between the facts that the judge had been missing. But, at the same time, the rationality of the historian shifts the rationality of the linking of the facts toward the rationality of their possibility.[4] It is therefore necessary for the law to outlaw the falsification of history. It is necessary, in short, for the law to do the work the historian cannot do, entrusted as they were with the job that the law cannot do.

This double aporia is, of course, only the mark of the law's and of science's adherence to a certain system of belief, the system of belief peculiar to the consensus system: realism. Realism claims to be that sane attitude of mind that sticks to observable realities. It is in fact something quite different: it is the police logic of order, which asserts, in all circumstances, that it is only doing the only thing possible to do. The consensus system has absorbed the historical and objective necessity of former times, reduced to the congruous portion of the "only thing possible" that the circumstances authorize. The possible is thereby the conceptual exchanger of "reality" and "necessity." It is also the final mode of "truth" that metapolitics perfected can offer the logic of the police order, the truth of the impossibility of the impossible. Realism is the absorption of all reality and all truth in the category of the only thing possible. In this logic, the possible/truth in all its scholarly authority is required to fill in all the holes in the possible/reality. The more unsteady the performances of managerial realism, the more it needs to legitimize itself through monotonous reiteration of the impossibility of the impossible, even if it means protecting this negative self-legitimization behind the thin barrier of the law that determines the point at which the emptiness of the truth must end, the limit that the argument of the impossibility of the impossible must not overstep. Hence the strange phenomenon of a law that outlaws the lie at a time when the law is trying to wipe out all the "taboos" that cut it off from a society itself devoted to infinite enjoyment of every sacrilege. What is at play here is not respect for the victims or holy terror but preservation of the flimsiest of secrets: the simple nullity of the impossibility of the impossible, which is the final truth of metapolitics and the ultimate legitimization of the managers of the only thing possible. More than it robs the negationists of speech, the ban rules out showing the simple emptiness of the argument of the unthinkable. There is absolutely nothing outside what is thinkable in the monstrousness of the Holocaust; nothing that goes beyond the combined capabilities of cruelty and cowardice when these benefit from all the means at the disposal of modern states; nothing these states are not capable of whenever there is a collapse in the forms of nonidentary subjectification of the count of the uncounted, wherever the democratic people is incorporated into the ethnic people.

No doubt Hannah Arendt's argument of the "banality of evil" leaves us intellectually dissatisfied. It has been criticized for banalizing the overwhelming hate aimed at a specific victim. But the argument is reversible. The Jewish identity eradicated by the Nazi extermination was no different from that of ordinary anti-Semitic fantasies. So it is indeed in the capacity to put together the means of extermination that the specific difference lies. Moreover, we do not need to be intellectually satisfied here. It is not a matter of explaining genocide. Clearly the problem has been put the wrong way around. Genocide is not a topical object that today impinges on our thinking with the effect of shaking up politics and philosophy. Rather, it is governmental curbing of politics, with its remainder or its humanitarian double, that has turned genocide into a philosophical preoccupation, engaging philosophy, as ethics, to somehow deal with what in this remnant the law and science cannot get at—that identity of the human and the inhuman that the consensus state has delegated to them to worry about. And it is from this standpoint that we should locate the discussion. No "good" explanation of genocide contrasts with the bad. Ways of locating the relationship between thought and the event of genocide either enter or fail to enter into the circle of the unthinkable.

The complexity of the play of this "unthinkable" is pretty well illustrated by a text of Jean-François Lyotard.[5] For Lyotard, any reflection on the Holocaust must deal with the specificity of the victim, the specificity of the plan to exterminate the Jewish people as a people who have witnessed an original debt of humanity toward the Other, thought's native impotence to which Judaism bears witness and which Greco-Roman civilization has always been keen to forget. But two ways of assigning thought to the event are inextricably intertwined in his demonstration. At first the issue seems to be about the type of memory or forgetting required by the event of genocide that has come to pass. It is then a matter of measuring the consequences the notion of genocide may have for Western philosophy's reconsideration of its history, without worrying about "explaining" genocide. But the moment this history is thought of in terms of repression, the name "Jew" becomes the name of the witness of this "forgotten" of which philosophy would like to forget the necessity of forgetting. The Holocaust then finds itself assigned the "philosophical" significance of the desire to get rid of what is repressed, by eliminating the sole witness to this condition of the Other as hostage, which is initially the condition of thought. The "philosophical" identity of the victim, of the witness/hostage, then becomes the reason for the crime. It is the identity of the witness of thought's impotence that the logic of a civilization demands be forgotten. And so we have the double knot of the powerfulness of the crime and the powerlessness of thought: on the one hand, the reality of the event is once again lodged in an infinite gap between the determination of the cause and the verification of the effect, and on the other hand, the demand that it be thought becomes the very place where thought, by confronting the monstrous effects of the denial of its own impotence, locks itself into a new figure of the unthinkable. The knot established between what the event demands of thought and the thought that commanded the event then allows itself to be caught up in the circle of ethical thinking. Ethics is thinking that hyperbolizes the *thought* content of the crime to restore thought to the memory of its native impotence. But ethics is also thinking that tars all thought and all politics with its own impotence, by making itself the custodian of the thought of a catastrophe from which no ethics, in any case, was able to protect us.[6]

Ethics, then, is the form in which "political philosophy" turns its initial project on its head. The initial project of philosophy was to eliminate politics to achieve its true essence. With Plato, philosophy proposed to achieve itself as the basis of the community, in place of politics, and this achievement of philosophy proved, in the final analysis, to mean elimination of philosophy itself. The social science of the nineteenth century was the modern manner in which the project of the elimination/realization of politics was achieved as realization/elimination of philosophy. Ethics is today the final form of this realization/elimination. It is the proposition put to philosophy to eliminate itself, to leave it to the absolute Other to atone for the flaws in the notion of the Same, the crimes of philosophy "realized" as soul of the community. Ethics infinitizes the crime to infinitize the injunction that it has itself addressed by the hostage, the witness, the victim: that philosophy atone for the old pretension of philosophical mastery and the modern illusion of humanity freed from alienation, that it submit to the regime of infinite otherness that distances every subject from itself. Philosophy then becomes the reflection of the mourning that now takes on evil as well as government reduction of *dikaïon* to *sumpheron*. In the name of ethics, it takes responsibility for evil, for the inhumanity of man that is the dark side of the idyll of consensus. It proposes a cure for the effacement of the political figures of otherness in the infinite otherness of the Other. It thus enlists in a perfectly determined relationship with politics—the one set out by Aristotle in the first book of *Politics* by separating political "humanity" from the twin figure of the stranger to the city: the subhuman or superhuman. The subhuman or superhuman is the monster or the god; it is the religious couple of the monstrous and the divine. Ethics sets thought up precisely in the face-to-face between the monster and the god,[7] which is to say that it takes on as its own mourning the mourning of politics.

Certainly one can only approve philosophy's present concern to be modest, meaning, conscious of the combined power and powerlessness of thought, of its puny power in relation to its own immoderation. It remains to be seen how this modest thinking is to be achieved in practice, the *mode* in which it claims to exercise its *moderation*. The present modesty of the state, as we have seen, is first of all modesty in relation to politics, in other words, hyperbolization of the normal practice of the state, which is to live off the elimination of politics. We should make sure that the modesty of philosophy is not also modesty at something else's expense, that it is not the final twist of this realization/elimination of politics that "political philosophy" lives off: the mourning of politics proclaimed as expiation of the faults of "realized" philosophy. There is no mourning of politics to be reflected upon, only its present difficulty and the manner in which this difficulty forces it to adopt a specific modesty and immodesty. Politics today must be immodest in relation to the modesty forced on it by the logics of consensual management of the "only thing possible." It must be modest in relation to the domain where it has been put by the immodest modesty of ethical philosophy: the domain of the immoderate remains of modest politics, meaning, the confrontation with naked humanity and the inhumanity of the human.

Political action finds itself today trapped in a pincer movement between state managerial police and the world police of humanitarianism. On the one hand, the logics of consensus systems efface the traces of political appearance, miscount, and dispute. On the other, they summon politics, driven from the scene, to set itself up from the position of a globalization of the human that is a globalization of the victim, a definition of a sense of the world and of a community of humanity based on the figure of the victim. On the one hand, they reduce the division involved in the count of the uncounted to a breakdown of groups open to presenting their identity; they locate the forms of political subjectivity within places of proximity (home, job, interest) and bonds of identity (sex, religion, race, culture). On the other, they globalize it, they exile it in the wilderness of humanity's sheer belonging to itself. They even recruit the very concern to reject the logics of consensus to imagine the basis of a non-identity-based community as being a humanity of the victim or hostage, of exile or of not belonging.

But political impropriety is not not belonging. It is belonging twice over: belonging to the world of properties and parts and belonging to the improper community, to that community that egalitarian logic sets up as the part of those who have no part. And the place of its impropriety is not exile. It is not the beyond where the human, in all its nakedness, would confront itself or its other, monster and/or divinity. Politics is not the consensual community of interests that combine. But nor is it the community of some kind of being-between, of an *interesse* that would impose its originarity on it, the originarity of a being-in-common based on the *esse* (being) of the *inter* (between) or the *inter* proper to the *esse*.[8] It is not the achievement of some more originally human humanity, to be reactivated within the mediocrity of the rule of interests or outside different disastrous embodiments. Politics' second nature is not the community's reappropriation of its original nature; it ought to be thought of effectively as second. The *interesse* is not the sense of community that the recapturing, in its originarity, of existence, being or "an alternative being," would deliver. The *inter* of a political *interesse* is that of an interruption or an interval. The political community is a community of interruptions, fractures, irregular and local, through which egalitarian logic comes and divides the police community from itself. It is a community of worlds in community that are intervals of subjectification: intervals constructed between identities, between spaces and places. Political being-together is a being-between: between identities, between worlds. Much as the "declaration of identity" of the accused, Blanqui, defined it, "proletarian" subjectification affirmed a community of wrong as an interval between a condition and a profession. It was the name given to beings situated between several names, several identities, several statuses: between the condition of noisy tool-wielder and the condition of speaking human being, between the condition of citizen and the condition of noncitizenship, between a definable social figure and the faceless figure of the uncounted. Political intervals are created by dividing a condition from itself. They are created by drawing a line between identities and places defined in a set place in a given world, and identities and places defined in other places and identities and places that have no place there. A political community is not the realization of a common essence or the essence of the common. It is the sharing of what is not given as being in-common: between the visible and the invisible, the near and the far, the present and the absent. This sharing assumes the construction of ties that bind the given to what is not given, the common to the private, what belongs to what does not belong. It is in this construction that common humanity argues for itself, reveals itself, and has an effect.

The simple relationship between humanity and its denial never creates a community of political dispute, as current events never cease to show us. Between exposure of the inhumanity suffered by the displaced or massacred populations of Bosnia, for example, and the feeling of belonging to common humanity, compassion and goodwill are not enough to knit the ties of a political subjectification that would include, in the democratic practice of the Western metropolises, a bond with the victims of Serb aggression or with those men and women resisting it. The simple feeling of a common essence and the wrong done to it does not create politics, not even particular instances of politics that would, for example, place a bond with the raped women of Bosnia under the banner of the women's movement. The construction of wrong as a bond of community with those who do not belong to the same common remains lacking. All the bodies shown and all the living testimonies to the massacres in Bosnia do not create the bond that was once created, at the time of the Algerian War and the anticolonialist movements, by the bodies, completely hidden from view and from any examination, of the Algerians thrown in the Seine by the French police in October 1961. Around those bodies, which disappeared twice, a political bond was effectively created, made up not of identification with the victims or even with their cause but of a disidentification in relation to the "French" subject who massacred them and removed them from any count. The denial of humanity was thus constructable within the local, singular universality of a political dispute, as French citizenry's litigious relationship with itself. The feeling of injustice does not go to make up a political bond through a simple identifying that would appropriate the disappropriation of the object of wrong. In addition, there has to be the disappropriation of identity that constitutes an appropriate subject for conducting the dispute. Politics is the art of warped deductions and mixed identities. It is the art of the local and singular construction of cases of universality. Such construction is only possible as long as the singularity of the wrong — the singularity of the local argument and expression of law — is distinguished from the particularization of right attributed to collectivities according to their identity. And it is also only possible as long as its universality is separate from the naked relationship between humanity and inhumanity.

The reign of globalization is not the reign of the universal. It is the opposite. It is in fact the disappearance of the places appropriate to its rationale. There is a world police and it can sometimes achieve some good. But there is no world politics. The "world" can get bigger. The universal of politics does not get any bigger. There remains the universality of the singular construction of disputes, which has no more to hope for from the newfound essence of a globalization more essentially "worldwide" than simple identification of the universal with the rule of law. We will not claim, as the "restorers" do, that politics has "simply" to find its own principle again to get back its vitality. Politics, in its specificity, is rare. It is always local and occasional. Its actual eclipse is perfectly real and no political science exists that could map its future any more than a political ethics that would make its existence the object solely of will. How some new politics could break the circle of cheerful consensuality and denial of humanity is scarcely foreseeable or de-cidable right now. Yet there are good reasons for thinking that it will not be able to get around the overblown promises of identity in rela-tion to the consensual logics of the allocation of parts or the hyper-bole that summons thought to a more original globalization or to a more radical experience of the inhumanity of the human.

Notes

All translations are by the translator unless otherwise stated.

Preface

1. Plato, *Gorgias*, 521 d (London: Penguin Classics, 1987).
2. Aristotle, *Politics*, III, 1282 b 21, trans. T. A. Sinclair, revised by Trevor J. Saunders (London: Penguin Classics, 1992), p. 207. [Other quotations from the *Politics* in this book are taken from this edition.— *Trans.*]
3. Jean-François Lyotard, *Le Différend* (Paris: Minuit, 1983); published in English translation as *The Differend: Phrases in Dispute,* trans. Georges Van Den Abbeele (Minneapolis: University of Minnesota Press, 1988).

1. The Beginning of Politics

1. Aristotle, *Politics,* I, 1253 a 9–17, p. 60.
2. Aristotle, *Politics,* III, 1281 b 36, p. 204.
3. Aristotle, *The Athenian Constitution,* 2, trans., intro., and annotated by P. J. Rhodes (London: Penguin Classics, 1984), p. 43.

4. Herodotus, *The Histories,* III, 80, 31, trans. George Rowlinson, ed. Hugh Bowden (London: Everyman, 1992), p. 258.

5. Aristotle, *Politics,* IV, 1294 a 19–20, p. 260.

6. Herodotus, *The Histories,* IV, 3, p. 296.

7. Plato, *Cratylus,* 417 d/e.

8. Aristotle, *Politics,* I, 1254 b 24–25, p. 69.

9. Plato, *The Republic,* IV, 434, trans. Sir Desmond Lee (London: Penguin Classics, 1987), p. 146.

2. Wrong

1. Pierre-Simon Ballanche, "Formule générale de l'histoire de tous les peuples appliquée à l'histoire du peuple romain," in *Revue de Paris,* September 1829, p. 94.

2. Ballanche, *"Formule générale,"* p. 75.

3. Michel Foucault, "*Omnes* et *singulatim:* vers une critique de la raison politique," in *Dits et Écrits,* vol. IV, pp. 134–61.

4. Jacques Rancière, *Le Maître ignorant* (Paris: Fayard, 1987); published in English as *The Ignorant Schoolmaster: Five Lessons in Intellectual Emancipation,* trans. and intro. by Kristin Ross (Stanford: Stanford University Press, 1991).

5. In *La Nuit des prolétaires* (Paris: Fayard, 1981), I have tried to show that it is also, at the same time, its loss, a going beyond in the sense of Nietzsche's *Untergang.* On the logic of speech events, let me refer you as well to my work *Les Noms de l'histoire* (Paris: Le Seuil, 1992). It seems to me this notion is connected to what Jean-Luc Nancy conceives as "taking the floor" in *Le Sens du monde* (Paris: Galilée, 1993). [These works are available in the following English translations: *The Nights of Labor: The Worker's Dream in Nineteenth-Century France,* trans. John Drury (Philadelphia: Temple University Press, 1989); *The Names of History: On the Poetics of Knowledge,* trans. Hassan Melehy (Minneapolis: University of Minnesota Press, 1994); *The Sense of the World,* trans. and with a foreword by Jeffrey S. Librett (Minneapolis: University of Minnesota Press, 1997). — *Trans.*]

6. *Défense du citoyen Louis-Auguste Blanqui devant la Cour d'assises* (Paris, 1832), p. 4.

3. The Rationality of Disagreement

1. Aristotle, *Politics,* I, 1254 b 5–26, p. 68 (also commented on in chapter 1).

2. Jürgen Habermas, "Sous le regard du troisième personne, que ce regard soit tourné vers l'extérieur ou vers l'intérieur, tout se gèle en objet," in *Le Discours philosophique de la modernité* (Paris: Gallimard, 1988), p. 352; published in English translation as *The Philosophical Discourses of Modernity: Twelve Lectures,* trans. F. Lawrence (Cambridge: Polity Press, 1987).

3. See Jean-François Lyotard, *Le Différend.*

4. "Réponse au manifeste des maîtres tailleurs," in *La Tribune politique et littéraire,* 7 November 1833.

5. "Réponse au manifeste des maîtres tailleurs."

6. Habermas, *Le Discours philosophique de la modernité,* p. 241 and following. This section is specifically devoted to a critique of Derridean deconstruction.

7. Immanuel Kant, *Critique de la faculté de juger* (Paris: Vrin, 1979), p. 50; published in English as *Critique of Judgement,* trans. J. H. Bernard (New York: Haffner, 1968).

8. Richard Rorty, *Contingency, Irony, and Solidarity* (Cambridge: Cambridge University Press, 1989).

4. From Archipolitics to Metapolitics

1. Plato, *The Laws,* VIII, 832 b/c, trans. and intro. by Trevor J. Saunders (London: Penguin Classics, 1975), p. 327. Compare with Plato, *The Republic,* IV, 445 c, p. 164.

2. See Plato, *The Republic,* II, 369 c 370 c, pp. 58–60. I offer an extended commentary on this passage in Jacques Rancière, *Le Philosophe des pauvres* (Paris: Fayard, 1983).

3. See Plato, *The Laws,* VII, 823 a, p. 318.

4. See Aristotle, *Politics,* II, 1261 a 41–42, p. 105.

5. Aristotle, *Politics,* IV, 1292 b 37–38, p. 255. For a more detailed analysis, see Jacques Rancière, *Aux bords de la politique* (Paris: Osiris, 1970).

6. See Aristotle, *Politics,* V, 1314 a–1315 b, pp. 346–51.

7. Thomas Hobbes, *On the Citizen* (Cambridge: Cambridge Texts in Political Thought, 1998), p. 69.

8. Hobbes, *On the Citizen,* p. 84.

5. Democracy or Consensus

1. See Claude Lefort, *Essais sur la politique* (Paris: Le Seuil, 1986); published in English translation as *Democracy and Political Theory,* trans. David Macey (Minneapolis: University of Minnsota Press, 1989).

2. See the works of Jean Baudrillard, in particular *L'Illusion de la fin* (Paris: Galilée, 1992); published in English translation as *The Illusion of the End,* trans. Chris Turner (Stanford: Stanford University Press, 1995).

3. See Gianni Vattimo, *La Société transparente* (Paris: Desclée de Brouwer, 1990); published in English translation as *The Transparent Society,* trans. David Webb (Baltimore: Johns Hopkins University Press, 1992).

6. Politics in Its Nihilistic Age

1. That it is necessary to send food and medicine to those in need and that people of remarkable skill and dedication are employed in these essential tasks is incontestable and I am not about to contest it here. What I am discussing is something else entirely: the subsuming of these categories in that of humanitarianism as the other side of state Realpolitik.

2. Paul Rassinier, *Le Mensonge d'Ulysse,* 2d ed. (Macon, 1955); published in English translation as *The Holocaust Story and the Lies of Ulysses* (Newport Beach, Calif.: Institute for Historical Renew, 1989).

3. Lucien Febvre, *Le Problème de l'incroyance au dix-septième siècle. La Religion de Rabelais* (Paris: Albin Michel, 1942); published in English translation as *The Problem of Unbelief in the Sixteenth Century: The Religion of Rabelais,* trans. Beatrice Gottlieb (Cambridge: Harvard University Press, 1985). For a more detailed analysis, see Jacques Rancière, "Les énoncés de la fin et du rien," *Traversées du nihilisme* (Paris: Osiris, 1993).

4. It is significant that it was a historian of ancient history, Pierre Vidal-Naquet, who led the fight against negationism in France, particularly with *Les Assassins de la mémoire* (Paris: La Découverte, 1970); published in English translation as *Assassins of Memory: Essays on the Denial of the Holocaust,* trans. Jeffrey Mehlman (New York: Columbia University Press, 1994). In order to ask what kind of truth the negationist provocations call upon, no doubt distance is necessary, the kind of distance familiarity with the antique notion of *pseudos* offers in relation to the historico-sociological rationality of attitudes and beliefs.

5. Jean-François Lyotard, *Heidegger et "les juifs"* (Paris: Galilée, 1988); published in English translation as *Heidegger and "the jews,"* trans. Andreas Michel and Mark Roberts, foreword by David Carroll (Minneapolis: University of Minnesota Press, 1990).

6. See Alain Badiou, *L'Ethique. Essai sur la conscience du mal* (Paris: Hatier, 1993).

7. Aristotle, *Politics,* I, 1253 a 5, p. 59.

8. This discussion could be taken further by referring to Jean-Luc Nancy's comments about politics as diffraction of the "in" of "in-common," especially in *La Comparution* (Paris: Christian Bourgois, 1991; published in English translation as *The Birth to Presence,* trans. Brian Holmes et al. [Standford: Stanford University Press, 1993]) and *Le Sens du monde (The Sense of the World).*

Index

Compiled by Hassan Melehy

Jacques Rancière is professor of aesthetics at the University of Paris-VIII (St. Denis). Three of his other books have also been translated into English: *The Nights of Labor: The Worker's Dream in Nineteenth-Century France* (1989), *The Ignorant Schoolmaster: Five Lessons in Intellectual Emancipation* (1991), and *The Names of History: On the Poetics of Knowledge* (Minnesota, 1994).

Julie Rose is a freelance writer and translator living in Australia.